Jack Simos

SOCIAL GROWTH
THROUGH PLAY PRODUCTION

ASSOCIATION PRESS

NEW YORK

SOCIAL GROWTH THROUGH PLAY PRODUCTION

Library of Congress catalog card number: 57-6885

 55

Printed in the United States of America
American Book–Stratford Press, Inc., New York

Dedicated
to my family—
Bertha, Mimi, and Mark Allen

Preface

A MAN'S BEHAVIOR, the development of his character and personality, his will to live and his will to die, are influenced in many ways. His way of life and his destiny can also be turned by certain dramatic events that take place during his lifetime.

The author's first contact with drama, back in the somber depression days of the '30's, constituted such an event for him. He had been a salesman and quite by chance had come into contact with the members of a "little theatre" group in the midwestern city where he lived. Having enjoyed their stimulating conversation, their pleasantries, and their extraordinary warmth and spontaneity, he soon responded to their pleas to become the business manager for the group.

It was at his first glimpse of a rehearsal that the great impact took place. A cast of twelve young men and women were seated circularly, discussing a line in a play—one line! It was not how to *say* the line that was the subject of intense controversy, but it was rather what the line *meant* that created the furor and the heated discussion.

Fascinating as it was to realize how so many different ideas could emanate from one line, the most striking impres-

sion upon the author was the complete absorption of the
would-be actors in the discussion. One could sense, one
could feel, around this one-line discussion alone the yearnings to be heard and the cravings to be recognized by each
individual. Here in the co-operative study of a single line
one could see a wedge thrust into the meaning of life, a
pathway formed from one individual to others, and a hope
born that life could have some dignity.

Added to the impact of this insight was another interesting phenomenon about this group which made a deep impression upon the author, namely, its heterogeneity. Here in
the same company were maids and clubwomen, an ex-prize
fighter and a librarian, factory workers and social workers,
mother and daughter, a minister and a butcher, young and
old—men and women all meeting on common ground. And
most of all, a director who made each one feel wanted, worth
while, and important.

How a drama group can give one this feeling of being important and worth while was realized by the author firsthand
when soon afterward he was asked to fill in a small part in
a play. At first reluctant, as acting had never occurred to him
even up to the time he had joined the group, the writer could
not resist the group pressure to help out in an emergency.

The character he was to play was that of an inept, rather
dull, stupid foreigner, but this description was true only at
a surface glance. As the analysis of the character by the
group began to take into account his past life and his future
potentialities, the realization took hold that probably at another more fortunate time and place he might even have
been a poet.

Over the years, there has been no waning of the writer's
first excitement in this special quality of drama that can help
people to grow in understanding. From prewar years of acting and directing, through four-and-one-half years of service,
to the postwar years where he joined the back-to-school

movement, his interest continued. The author obtained a B.S. Degree in Education, with a major in Drama and then, still fascinated by the human relations potentials of drama, moved into graduate work in Social Work, where some of the material in this book first made its appearance as a Master's Thesis. And in the past six years of work in children's institutions, the philosophy and techniques of creative play directing stood him in good stead, whether he was involved in play direction itself or in the supervision, teaching, and training of house parents in the art of helping unhappy children feel wanted, worth while and important.

The audacity to write a book comes not only from the writer's own compelling urge to share his conviction in the value of the use of drama for those working in the various fields dealing with human relations but also from the encouragement he has received from friends and colleagues who have read the original Master's Thesis and who have seen some of the examples to be illustrated in this book.

The book is written, therefore, from the vantage point of the author's own profession, social work, his specialization, social group work, and his own program forte, drama. It is written, however, not for social workers alone but for all those concerned with ideas and methods of helping people to become more adequate and to realize more fully their own potentials—social workers, educators, psychologists, psychiatrists, recreation leaders, and the many publicly responsible citizens who have been increasingly concerned with the problems of mental illness, juvenile delinquency, and emotional disturbance in our ever more complicated society.

This book is written for those who are already directing plays—the community center play director, the English and speech teacher in high school, the college drama director and drama teacher—those who desire that drama for the amateur should be an experience of growth as well as entertainment, and for whom the deep and lasting experiences their pupils gain are altogether as important as the production itself.

It is presented also for drama students who are motivated by an interest in people and in creative expression, who might be the future social dramatists and who might desire to use their skills in teaching and directing in the schools and in the social service field, the community center, the mental hospital, the children's treatment center, and in all places where people gather to seek social outlets.

And, finally, in order that they may see firsthand what is involved in producing a play creatively directed, as well as what benefits may be derived therefrom, this book is submitted to the leisure-time agency executive, the program director, the social group worker, the camp director, the minister, the recreation department head, the school principal —all those who have a voice in determining the program diet and program priorities of an agency, school, or institution.

The approach to be used in this book is that of getting down to cases. Included will be the example of a total play production, showing the step-by-step process and techniques of direction and acting used. Another play production will be analyzed in order to study cases of actual people and the significance to them of participation in such a project.

Our first chapter deals with the relationship of drama to the problem of human relations. The second chapter sets forth the theory of a creative approach to drama, upon which the writer's method is based. Our final chapters are a recapitulation in greater detail of drama experiences with the focus on identifying the specific benefits and values to be gained from this activity.

Acknowledgments

The book is an attempt to show how directing a play, acting a part, studying human behavior and life in the process of ferreting out the meanings of the lines in the play, are interests which cut across many fields of activity. A certain degree of kinship between the field of drama and various fields of human relations will be seen. To the writer this book is an integration of ideas and experiences dating back some twenty years. To attempt acknowledgment of the many people who had an influence and effect upon such an integration would be an impossible task, but the writer would like to pick out for special thanks a few of the persons who have been most helpful.

To Dr. Morris (Fritz) Mayer, resident director of Belle-faire, residential treatment center for emotionally disturbed children in Cleveland, Ohio, with whom the author has been closely associated for the past five years both professionally and personally, he expresses his gratitude for the many ideas and suggestions he has received. The section on "The Use of the Spoken Word" as well as the techniques around the use of anticipation would not have come about without his guidance and stimulation. To Dr. William Weinstein, former instructor of Social Group Work at the School of Applied Social Sciences, Western Reserve University, and now with the Jewish Association of Neighborhood Centers, New York City, go special thanks for reading and editing the first draft of this manuscript, keeping the author in tow and preventing him from going out on tangents. The author expresses his appreciation also to Reuben Silver, Director of Drama at Karamu House, Cleveland, for his help on the chapter which is entitled "Selecting the Play." To Margaret Golton, social case work supervisor at Bellefaire, Dr. David Crocker, staff psychiatrist at Bellefaire, and Sylvia Feldblum, case worker at the Jewish Family Service Association of Cleveland, go grateful acknowledgment for their reading of the manuscript and the helpful analyses and encouragement they offered. To Sidney Wasserman, former actor, now a social case worker at Bellefaire, and Margaret Schwartz, supervisor of the sewing room at Bellefaire, go thanks for their technical help with make-up and costuming in producing the play, "Golden Boy."

The writer also wishes to express his appreciation to his former colleagues and to the faculty of the School of Social Work and of the University Theatre of the University of Minnesota for their interest and help in the preparation of the original Master's Thesis. To his former social work adviser, Mrs. Gisela Konopka, go special thanks for her indispensable aid with focusing and clarifying the diversified concepts and material here contained. And to a former stimulating drama teacher, Dr. Kenneth Graham, a leader in the art of Creative Dramatics for children, also goes appreciation for his help in reading the original Master's Thesis. Acknowledgment is made to Bryce Shoemaker, former instructor of Philosophy and Speech at Augsburg College, Minneapolis, Minnesota, and now a Lutheran pastor in that city, for his co-operation in the production of the play, "A Christmas Carol."

Most of all, the boys and girls of Bellefaire deserve commendation, for it was through their efforts that the writer was sustained in his conviction that given opportunity and faith, people will rise to the challenge.

Thanks would not be complete, however, without acknowledging the writer's indebtedness to two old friends and colleagues with whom he analyzed that all-important first line. To Jack Geller, now of Chicago, Illinois, who taught the writer the art of directing plays creatively, and to Donald Singerman of the Hill Reference Library, St. Paul, Minnesota, who worked with him for many years in the development of the creative approach, the writer takes this opportunity to express his deep gratitude.

JACK SIMOS

Contents

The Age of Integration . . . Therapy Versus Social Growth . . . Play Production and Psychodrama . . . Dangers of Play Production

"My First Play" . . . Internal Techniques . . . "Therapeutic" Casting . . . Artistic Success . . . Professional Versus Amateur

Rehearsal 1. Understanding the Play . . . Rehearsals 2 and 3. Studying the Characters, Working for Naturalness, Digging into Meanings, Breaking Up Lines into Thoughts . . . Rehearsals 4 and 5. Associating Meanings with Movement (Blocking) . . . Rehearsal 6. Blending and Refining Meanings and Motivations with Movements and Characterization, Taking Scenes Apart and Putting Them Together . . . Rehearsal 7. The Actor as a Whole, Acting and Reacting, Blending In of Lines

Drama and Human Relations

A SEVEN-YEAR-OLD GIRL climbs up a tree. Her cheeks are rosy; she glows with excitement. Halfway up she comes to a halt. "Whoo-whoo!" she sings out. She is the engineer on a train. She waves her arm in a signal to a nine-year-old lad, who is busy on the porch, soberly stoking coal into a red-hot furnace.

In a basement playroom a mat is spread. It is a barn. A group of young boys and girls are prancing around, neighing like horses. An older boy stands guard. One of the horses strays from its stall. "Ho, there, Dobbin," challenges the guard, as he pulls it back to its place in the barn.

An adult walks three boys to school. During the trip, one of the children, flushed with anticipation, suddenly turns to the adult and says, "You're a big boat, and I'm a little tug boat." He grabs the adult's hand. "I'm tugging you out to sea," he explains, pulling the adult along, and both break into a trot. "Yeah, yeah," chime in the other two youngsters, as one grabs the other hand of the adult, while the third pushes from the rear.

Who among us has not at some time observed similar evidences of this dramatic impulse? Such an impulse, the impulse to play-act, to act out, is indeed universal. From the beginnings of civilization—since the first spoken word—to the present time, in one form or another, drama has played a vital, enriching role in society.

How drama can be used today, how the play-acting impulse can be harnessed to help people grow, to develop greater sensitivity to themselves and to their fellow human beings, to become more spontaneous and outgoing, to discard old fears and insecurities, has attracted the interest of many who are working in the various fields of human relations. They are on the constant look-out for new forms of activity which can help to build good relations among human beings and can act as a prevention as well as a cure to personality breakdown. Consequently, new forms of drama have developed, such as creative dramatics, puppetry, role playing and psychodrama, whereby experiments have been made with an eye to the effect on the individual's personality development and social growth and not on the performance alone.

The most recent revelation of such a new form of drama is presented in Peter Slade's *Child Drama,* in which he demonstrates most vividly the values of play-making artistry for children from birth to fifteen years, as found in schools in England.

Sybil Thorndike, eminent British actress, comments in her spirited foreword to his book,

> ". . . what Peter Slade has done for children I believe the theatre should be doing for grown-up children—for ordinary human beings. . . ." [1] *

Experiments with play production for grown-ups are already taking place, especially in mental hospitals. One notable example of the use of "The Caine Mutiny Court-Martial" in the Veterans Administration Hospital in Salt Lake

---

* Editor's note: All footnotes appear at the end of chapters.

City, Utah, has been called to our attention by *Time* Magazine.[2]

This writer starts, in a sense, where Peter Slade leaves off. *Social Growth Through Play Production* deals with the age group from thirteen years and up. Moreover, not a new form of drama is presented here but, rather, a new approach to a form as old as civilization itself. This approach to the conventional proscenium type of drama, however, is quite similar in its philosophy to the sincere, spontaneous, improvisation forms of drama embodied in the play-making techniques of Peter Slade and Winifred Ward.

The Age of Integration

We have come from an age of specialization to an age of integration. Biology and chemistry have merged into the field of biochemistry. Physical education and medicine have combined into physical medicine. The very teaching of medicine has changed from its focus on disease to a focus on the total person, aided by specializations such as psychiatry. Psychiatry is also included in the curricula of ministerial students.

The study of human relations draws its material from many sources—psychology, psychiatry, sociology, history, social work, education, and many others. Drama as it will be discussed here will be seen not only as a beneficial recreational activity but also as another rich source from which to draw knowledge of human behavior. For drama, like the fields listed above, deals with the dynamics of human behavior. As the great critic, Ferdinand Brunetière, expressed it:

"... Drama is the representation of the will of man in conflict with the mysterious powers or natural forces which limit and belittle us; it is one of us thrown living upon the stage there to struggle against fatality, against social law, against one of his fellow mortals, against himself, if need be, against

the ambitions, the interests, the prejudices, the folly, the malev-
olence of those who surround him." [3]

Since the nature of the actor's activity is in his learning
to portray a character realistically, the writer believes that
if the character in the play is a true representation of life
and struggle—a prerequisite for any good play—the participant stands to gain from his study of the character a deeper
understanding of the world and of people. Furthermore, the
nature of this activity could afford a circuitous route to the
ultimate understanding by the participant of his own struggles and conflicts. At least his participation in the process
of studying and portraying the true life struggle of a character could act as a catalytic agent toward motivating him
to examine his own. To see that all people have problems
and struggles, victories and defeats, virtues and faults, could
help a person to see that he is not so different from others.
The nature of this activity of drama, at any rate, lends to
the program medium of dramatics a unique third-dimensional
quality in its focus on human behavior which endows it with
special values not found in the usual program tools which
we associate with recreational activities. It is the writer's
contention, which will be elaborated in the pages to follow,
that this unique quality of drama deserves a great deal of
study and experiment in relation not only to its value in
general growth and enrichment of living but also to its re-
educational and curative potentials.

Therapy Versus Social Growth

There would be great danger, however, in thinking of the
techniques here to be demonstrated as "group therapy." Our
frame of reference for the word "therapy" is that technique
which addresses itself directly to helping a person with his
own problems. World War II saw the development of therapy from a strictly individual to a group form, based on the

large number of men needing help with emotional problems and breakdowns, the comparative scarcity of specialists qualified to give such help, and the similarity of symptoms and problems. Eventually, aside from the original use of this group approach for reasons of expediency, other specific values were discovered in its application that warranted a further pursuit of the technique.

It is the writer's belief that a person's participation in a play also can have curative and therapeutic effects, but these are brought about by the ego building he receives from the experience and from the stimulation he gets to examine his own life objectively and to see his common bond with his fellow man.

Getting a person to express to the group or the group leader his own involvement in a problem is an aim of therapy and is not an objective of this book. Only those who have the professional skill and the professional assignment have the right to engage in this kind of endeavor. Not only is "a little knowledge . . . a dangerous thing," but curiosity without compassion can be cruel and terrible. We shall point out, in the examples to be given, the line dividing the kind of personal discussion between the director and the cast, which is dictated by the interests of successful artistic play production, from the kind of discussion which would constitute irresponsible probing and psychoanalytic dabbling. The creative method of play directing makes use of the free-association techniques of psychoanalysis, but it does not have the same goals. Because of the similarity in techniques, however, double caution must be exerted to prevent treading into the area of therapy.

Play Production and Psychodrama

There is a form of drama called psychodrama which does have therapy as its goal. In this technique situations are structured in such a way as to enable the patients to act out directly their own experiences, to enact roles relating directly to their own problems, and to use words and lines of their own making. In play production the actor does the opposite. He must adapt himself to a role already set and learn the meanings of lines already created by the author.

This book on play production will not only identify the process of the actor's adaptation of himself to the dictates of the play but will also show how through such a process one can gain a better image of one's self, a clearer insight into life, and a deeper knowledge of the art of human relations. Again, this approach is in no way a substitute for psychodrama, nor the specialized media of role playing, puppetry, playmaking, and creative dramatics.

Dangers of Play Production

Although there is more than one approach to the production of a play, great stress will be laid here upon a creative approach based upon and adapted from the drama theories of Constantin Stanislavski.[4]

If production of formal plays is to bring about real personal and social development, it is essential that the approach in the direction be creative and not rigid, for there can be dangers in play production when directed mechanically or lackadaisically. The case against such play production is stated quite succinctly by S. R. Slavson in the following:

> The appeal of the ordinary dramatic performance is almost entirely to egocentric interests such as exhibitionism, self-assertion, power, desire to attract attention, to occupy the center of the stage, to make believe as an escape from reality. Again, the superficiality with which the youthful actors represent characters in plays leads to half-learning and confusion. They do not acquire any understanding of the character's problems. They do not learn to appreciate his conflicts, or grasp the significance of the plot and dramatic situation. This type of dramatics encourages superficial thinking and unsympathetic

response to others. Character education, on the contrary, ought to emphasize sincerity and honesty, thoughtfulness, insight, and sympathy—characteristics that are not engendered by mere impersonation.[5]

There is a great deal of merit in such apprehensiveness of the dangers of drama, for all too frequently the way in which amateur plays are directed and performed today bears out such criticism.

We hope to illustrate how actors can be taught and directed to represent characters realistically and not superficially, how they can acquire understanding of a character's problem, and how they can be taught not only to understand reality but also how to express it through their own emotions and their own feelings, thus obtaining a true emotional release and subsequently a richer appreciation of the reality world surrounding them.

The greatest value to be derived from the creative approach is in *the possibility it offers in recognizing that what the individual feels and believes is important*—a basic aim of mental hygiene. It accomplishes this by demonstrating in words and by actions the inherent value and dignity of the individual. In discussing the creative approach, and in the subsequent illustrations, we hope to show how this can be achieved.

FOOTNOTES

1. Peter Slade, *Child Drama* (Warwick Square, London, E.C.4: University of London Press, Ltd., 1954), p. 5.

2. *Time* Magazine, March 28, 1955, pp. 94-95.

3. Reprinted from *Producing the Play,* Revised, by John Gassner, by permission of The Dryden Press, Inc. Copyright 1953 by The Dryden Press. The excerpt cites Ferdinand Brunetière in "The Law of the Drama," p. 16.

4. As background, it might be well to mention that Constantin Stanislavski was a former actor and director of the Moscow Art Theatre, which has achieved world-wide recognition as an outstanding theatre organization.

5. S. R. Slavson, *Creative Group Education* (New York: Association Press, 1938), p. 114.

CHAPTER TWO

A Creative Approach

IN THE SPRING OF 1948 the writer directed the play "The Beautiful People" by William Saroyan with a cast of almost totally inexperienced people before an audience of about three hundred in a Jewish Community Center. The cast was composed, principally, of high school seniors. At the cast party following the performance, the boy who had played the part of Jonah Webster was prevailed upon to read an English theme he had written in connection with this, his first experience acting in a play. Let him give his idea of the creative approach:

"My First Play"

It's not the performance. It's the thousand and one things that make the performance. It's those first tryouts when you're so eager to make the right impression on the director. It's that wonderful feeling when you know you've won a part. Then it's rehearsals. The camaraderie that passes between the cast, the groping for your characterization—then it's learning your lines and feeling the things that the author felt when he wrote them. Then it's realization . . . you're not playing a part; you're becoming another human being. . . . Then comes discouragement you can never be someone else even for a play. The discouragement is replaced by determination . . . it's your part and you'll do it. Then it's drive and work and sudden awakening—the performance is a week away and you're not ready. You'll never be ready—the part's just too big. Why were you picked? The regrets bring on resolves—the director has worked so hard and taught you so much, and he believes in you—you can't let him down. And what about the rest of the cast? They face the same troubles, why can't you? You do. It means something to you now. You realize how much you've enjoyed everything even the "drudgery" and you realize how far you've come. You dream about the play . . . you didn't realize you were that preoccupied with it. Nothing else is important. School is forgotten . . . as is everything. . . . Now nothing matters but performance. A hundred details spring up at once. Your costume, wig, tickets—and you've lost your script. Then suddenly the nervous tension leaves and a lethargy sets in. It shows on stage. Everything seems to be wrong. You're mentally stale. You stay that way till dress rehearsal, then you put forth your best effort. You get the director's notes after rehearsal. It's discouraging. You didn't imagine you made so many mistakes.

It's the day before the play now. You have the day off to relax. You do. You didn't think you would. But you're perfectly relaxed. The time slowly slips away.

Then the performance. You don't feel nervous . . . you wonder why. You begin to josh around with the cast. You don't know what to do. You walk around and around the make-up room. Then the play goes on. You feel tight for the actors on stage. Now it's almost time to go on. You take your position and begin to check your props. You've got everything. There's your cue—you gulp and say to yourself, "I'm entering my own home . . . those are my children. . . . Be old, be dignified. . . . Be Jonah Webster." Then you enter. Everything is so familiar. It's just like those tens of rehearsals. You bring yourself back to the play . . . and smile to yourself for you've done everything right without even thinking about it. You feel sure of yourself now. A prop isn't in place—it doesn't bother

you. Now the lines are coming . . . you're acting—you don't
feel like you're acting, and you don't feel like Jonah either.
You look at the girl on stage with you and keep saying to yourself, "She's your daughter . . . Be tender." Then the scene is
ending . . . your punch lines are coming up. Suddenly you're
Jonah. You don't remember the audience. You don't remember
you're acting. You don't even remember your lines, but they
keep coming smooth and true. Then the act is over. Techni-
cians pour onto the stage. . . . You feel limp, everyone is hurry-
ing around looking for something, doing something, and you
feel limp. Someone speaks to you. You aren't listening. You
try to remember what was said. You concentrate hard on
remembering and you forget about Jonah and become yourself. Then the second act is starting. You try to regain Jonah.
You say your lines. But you're not Jonah. You don't worry
about it. You know it will come as in the first act. But it
doesn't. The scene is done. And you break while the stage is
set for the finale. This is it. If the last scene is right, the whole
thing will go over. The curtain goes up. You're doing the right
things but you don't feel right. Something is missing. You keep
searching for it—you never do find it because now the play is
ending. You feel disgusted . . . you haven't grasped your part
yet. Then the curtain goes down. The applause roars in. You
hear it. But it doesn't make you feel good. You hurry off stage
feeling empty and disgusted. You want to get your make-up
off and go home. Then the mob bursts backstage. Smiling,
fawning people hover around you and shout their praises:
"Wonderful, terrific!"—meaningless words. You look right
into their eyes . . . and they seem sincere. You feel like laughing in their poor, dumb faces, but you just nod your head and
smile obsequious "thank you's." It's the best acting you've
done all night.

Then you're going home. There is talk around you, but
you're alone with your mind. You ask, "Was it worth it?"
You think back to those late rehearsals . . . to the little incidents at those rehearsals . . . and you find yourself smiling
and you know you enjoyed every minute of it. Remember the
time Manny brought the "Rat Trap"? You laugh. You begin

to feel good all over. Suddenly you want to do another play—you'd get it this time. It's a challenge and you want to accept it. You wish there were a play open now so you could pitch right in. You can see all your mistakes now. You'd know how to attack the part. If you'd known this much when you took your first part, you wouldn't feel empty now. You've got to create the character . . . that's the only way you can be the character. You just listened to the director and tried to portray the part he created, but you can't feel satisfied portraying anything but your own. No wonder you felt empty. Your SELF wasn't there. You know what was wrong. You've found what was missing. Now you want to try again because acting is in your blood.[1]

It is true that except for a few moments, when he suddenly became Jonah and forgot he was acting, this young man had not yet grasped his part. In the realization of this fact, he showed an awareness that he had not had an artistic success. This very realization, this very dissatisfaction, makes it quite clear that he was not motivated by egocentric interests such as listed by Slavson. If success had been measured by such criteria, his would have been outstanding, for there was no lack of applause and praise. But it was the fully creative experience which he wanted and which was his criterion for success.

An important point here is that this amateur actor may not have started out with this aim in mind. Indeed, he could very well have begun with egocentric motives, with his desire to impress not only the director but also the audience. But here we see a basic principle of modern education applied: to start where the group or the individual is. In the process of his struggle to understand the play, create the character, and work together with his fellow cast members, this individual's objectives and aims were broadened and his values heightened. This is in itself successful social growth. And though the writer will continually be stressing the importance of working for artistic success, we can see, however, that from the point of view of growth in insight, into character development, group loyalty and bond, satisfactory relationships and personal achievement, the experience was definitely not a failure, for the actor came out of the experience with a true grasp of the essence of the creative approach—his own *self* had to be there. He "could never be anyone else even for a play." The concept of the self is the opposite of "impersonation," a pitfall to be avoided in drama.

The results—though imperfect—that can be gleaned from this boy's writing, had been obtained by the use of techniques and skills inspired by the philosophy of creativity originated by Constantin Stanislavski. Among some of the well-known theatre organizations which followed the so-called Stanislavski method was the Group Theatre of New York. A cursory glance at a few of the objectives of this organization when it began in 1931 suggests a certain kinship to the field of human relations.

> To achieve a fuller realization of the individual actor's life.
> To rehearse each play unhurriedly, carefully, beginning with detailed discussions of the meaning or "spine" of the play until a common interpretation is agreed upon by author, director, executives, actors, scene designer, etc.[2]

Stanislavski's term for this method is the organic approach, both from the standpoint of the play itself being unified around a "spine" or "seed" and from the point of view of the acting being that of the whole person. This approach represented a sharp break with the teaching of the past, which emphasized "elements of physical expression,"—body, voice, gestures, stage devices, etc.[3] These latter are, perhaps, the techniques of impersonation.

Those working in the field of human relations know, for example, that acceptance of an individual cannot be communicated merely by using an external device such as patting one on the arm or smiling. The person as a whole must show this acceptance in order to be convincing. His feelings and attitudes, which are internal, can easily belie, or at least fail to support, the external show of acceptance. And when this happens, no matter how accomplished this external technique—the pat on the arm—may be, the conveyance of acceptance will not be convincing.

Unfortunately, the emphasis in most of our present-day acting lies on such external techniques as patting on the arm, stereotyped gesturing, bodily expressions, posture, and proper diction. There is, in fact, a list of examples of bodily language listed in Crafton and Royer's book, *The Complete Acted Play,* which lends credence to the importance that external techniques play in modern acting, and which has, undoubtedly, called forth Slavson's opposition:

> . . . Good feeling is expressed by erect posture, head up and chin out. . . .
> . . . Mental depression is suggested by half-closed eyes, a relaxed body, drooping shoulders, lifeless arms, and limp hands.
> . . . Fear may be expressed by having the actor stand with one foot in advance of the other, the weight of the body resting on the rear foot, one hand raised across the body, palm down, with fingers spread and slightly bent; chest back, head slightly down and forward, eyes wide, and lips slightly parted. . . . [4]

In fairness to Crafton and Royer, it should be pointed out that this list was intended by the authors to constitute only "one instrument for acting." [5] They acknowledge that "there must be a harmony between the physical on the one hand and the mental and spiritual on the other." [6] But even such a postulation would run counter to the concept of organic action of the person as a whole. Since every person is different, and if he is to act as a whole person, every expression of good feeling, depression, or fear will be unique. In discussing the emotion of fear, for example, I. Rapoport says:

There are as many individual instances of fear as there are people.

It is one thing to be frightened by a frog which jumps up before one's foot, and quite another thing to be frightened by an explosion. A young girl's fright differs from that of a healthy lad. Every person has his own individual expression of this or that feeling under any given set of circumstances.

It is therefore impossible to act feelings "in general." One must perform the task which will evoke the specific feeling.[7]

Internal Techniques

How, then, can we express emotion that is specific, lifelike and genuine? The great contribution of Stanislavski is his provision of *internal* techniques by which the actor is enabled to act as *he* would if *he* were caught in the same web of circumstances and confronted with the same obstacles as the character.

Memory Recall

Go back to nature, is the essence of the Stanislavski formula. By nature he means one's own experiences. In order to express a certain feeling that seems to be called for on the stage, one should go back and use one's memory recall for an experience of one's own in which one felt similarly. This technique is called by various terms—memory recall, affect memory, memory of emotion. One should recall, however, not the emotion but rather the stimuli that evoked the emotion.

One should not try to remember feelings, but rather the physical details and the circumstances which produced the feeling.[8] In real life our feelings come in spite of ourselves. An elderly lady, for example, seated at her dining-room table, talking about her late husband, starts musing quite matter-of-factly. It was four o'clock in the morning, on a Sunday. She can remember it as plain as day. She had been restless and unable to sleep. As she goes on with the further details—the weather, the house she lived in, the supper menu, all the small details surrounding the incident of her husband's death—her feelings return, her eyes begin to water, and she is filled with nostalgic sadness.

Doing—Not Pretending

In the final analysis, the essence of acting is to reduce emotion to some manageable size, to some elementary bits of action. Acting is not pretending but doing. Sudakov expresses it in this way:

> If you analyze human life, you will see that it can be resolved into a series of actions which are simple and can be easily executed. . . . No sooner does the actor come out upon the stage to enact a part that is packed with intense feeling than he seizes upon those feelings, trying to act them out, and thus foredooms himself to clichés which inevitably distort the nature of his acting. Feelings should never be forced. One should ask himself: what would one do, what simple action would he perform if he found himself in despair; if, for example, he were rejected by the girl whom he loved or if he were to vacate an apartment for failure to pay his rent. In such cases he would start doing something or at least he would begin thinking about some plan of action . . . how to arrange one's affairs, what to do about one's debts, where to put up one's family. What I might feel—this should not even be answered. To think of what I might have thought, said or done in such a case—that is the best way of making oneself have that inner experience. To think of how I might feel in any given situation is the surest way of falling into the beaten track of affected acting . . . [9]

Doesn't this same theory hold true in such human relations work as social case work or counseling where a worker may get at the real feeling of her client by reconstructing the event in its simple, specific details? Let us look at a case record which illustrates this point. The details and background do not matter. Let us see just how the case worker and the client lead into the expression of emotion.

> ". . . I asked what the difficulty was and could she tell us a little more about it.
>
> "She said quickly that he seemed to be a good boy and she thought that he was not really bad. He has no difficulty outside the house. He is liked in school and gets along quite nicely. Last year he had to repeat a class because he did not do his homework, but this year he is getting along. He got his report card yesterday and he received B's in all subjects, but in his behavior he had B plus. He is well liked in the church and he has a lot of friends who like him too. All the trouble is at home.
>
> "All the trouble is with her. He hates her and he tells her so. *She began to cry and buried her head in her hands.* . . . If she tells him that he should come home at about seven or eight at night, he does not do it, but comes home much later. If she wants him to go to bed he deliberately walks outside of the house, stays out five minutes, and then comes back to go to bed, just to show her he can do whatever he wants to. I asked *what Mrs. Gonzales did* when Tony behaved like this. Well, she has tried all different kinds of methods. At first she slapped him, then tried to be strict with him and punish him, but this has no effect whatsoever. Now she doesn't do anything any more. She *shrugged her shoulders,* resignedly. What can she do? . . ." [10] (Italicizing is the writer's.)

It will be noted that the case worker does not ask how the client feels but rather what she does in the situation described. This principle of evoking an emotion by getting at the specific actions also holds true in the creative approach to drama.

Though a thorough discussion of the creative approach would require far more time and space than can be allotted here, a few other aspects of internal techniques should be mentioned, since it is by these very techniques that many of the values to be discussed later can be obtained.

Inner Motivation

One of these aspects is that of inner justification, some-times called motivation from within. Motivation in drama is the concept that every action on the stage must have a reason. If a character is to walk from one side of the stage to the other and there doesn't seem to be a good reason, one can be invented—such as to empty his pipe. This is motivation on a superficial level. Inner motivation goes deeper. Under this concept it would be necessary to determine *why* the character empties his pipe at that point, anyway. Is he embarrassed? Is he stalling for time to muster his thoughts in the face of some new facts that have just been revealed? Under such a concept inner justification must be found even for standing still.

The diligent use of inner justification in a play should be an adequate preventative against the danger of developing "onesidedness of characterization" and "half-learning." Constant inquiries of *why* the character acts the way he does and the constant reasoning out of the appropriateness of movement should lead, ultimately, to an awareness of hitherto unsuspected motives underlying actions. The more the play is related to life, of course, the more related will be the actor's awareness of motives underlying actions of everyday existence. Thus will the basis be laid for a sympathetic and sensitive understanding of his fellow men, which is social growth.

It is one thing to understand motivations; it is quite another thing, however, to act them out upon a stage in front of an audience.

Self-Consciousness

How can the actor keep from becoming self-conscious in front of an audience? The answer, found in the creative approach, is concentration on the *content* rather than on the form—or what Rapoport calls organic attention.[11] In real life a person's attention is always focused on something. Even when he rests, thoughts flow through his mind. On the stage, the more the actor can be absorbed and engrossed in the content of what he is saying, the sooner will he lose his consciousness of appearing before an audience. And when he is not talking, the focus of his attention is on what is being said or on some specific object—listening and reacting to the situation. The extent to which he becomes interested in the object of his attention, the more he looks at it, weighs it and wonders about it, the more organic his attention will be and the more human and lifelike he will appear to the audience.[12] The greater the development of such skill, the less the danger of egocentricity, the less concern with the impression being made on the audience (as seen too often in the furtive side-glances cast over the footlights by amateur actors trained in external techniques). As our young theme writer states, "Suddenly you're Jonah. You don't remember the audience. You don't remember you're acting. . . ."

Stage Interinfluence

Closely connected with the concept of concentration and attention is that of stage interinfluence. According to Rapoport:

> Stage interinfluence we can define as the influence of the players on one another under the conditions of an indissoluble interrelationship between them when the least change in the behavior of one inevitably brings with it a corresponding change in the behavior of the other, and vice versa. . . . This vital law of interinfluence, inner relations and their mutual influence on each other between people must be understood and transferred to the stage. . . . Here it is important to understand that we must talk to each other, as required by the play, not in a formal fashion, not by means of memorized external movements, but organically, on the basis of living relationships between people.[13]

This is the same concept that social group workers know as psychic interaction.

Is it being said that all there is to creativity is to be ourselves? That would, indeed, make the task quite simple. Unfortunately, there is more than this needed by an actor. The art of creating includes that of being highly selective. Stanislavski describes the art with understanding:

> . . . an artist does not build his role out of the first thing at hand. He chooses very carefully among his memories and culls out of his living experiences the ones that are most enticing . . . an artist takes the best that is in him and carries it over on the stage. . . . He may not have in his nature either the villainy of one character or the nobility of another, but the seeds of those qualities will be there because we have in us the elements of all human characteristics, good and bad. An actor should use his art and his technique to discover, by natural means, those elements which it is necessary for him to develop for his part.[14]

"Therapeutic" Casting

It is most important to realize that an actor should not attempt to portray personality qualities on the stage which he does not possess as a person. We call attention to this because some of our mental hygienists in their eagerness to achieve therapeutic gains have gone so far as to advocate a deliberate miscasting of individuals in parts that do not fit their own physical characteristics or temperaments. One mental hygienist, for example, has favored giving the part of an aggressive, shouting boss to a shy, withdrawn youngster in the hope that this would stimulate him into becoming more aggressive.[15] This type of casting has been characterized by an educator as an attempt at "bailing the sea with a spoon."[16] Behavior cannot be changed this easily. Though we shall be devoting an entire chapter to the subject of "The

Player and the Part," we should, perhaps, present our point of view by an illustration at this time drawn from an incident in the writer's experience.

Cantankerous Curly

Back in 1939 the theatre group of which the writer was business manager was in the process of rehearsing a one-act play, "Count the Days I'm Gone," by Frank Keyser. Since no one else was available, an actor was selected for a part who was far from resembling that character in physique, temperament, or personality. The character was that of Curly, a hardened, insensitive, agile, strong, tough sailor. He grumbled and swore continually and pushed people aside. He was bold and blustering and threatening. On the other hand, the actor had just concluded enacting the role of an inept, confused naïve storekeeper in one play and an old, philosophical grandfather in another. The praise he had received for his enactment of these roles gave him the cockiness to undertake this one.

He started off as one might expect if one looked at a tough sailor with stereotyped characteristics. He threw his shoulders back, hoisted his chest, strutted about, primped, talked out of the side of his mouth, and yelled. After a few days the director gravely pronounced his verdict: artificial, inconsequential, false!

That night, after the others had left, the director and actor stayed over. "We are going to see what is in you that is in Curly or could be in Curly. What doesn't fit we'll eliminate," was the director's opening comment.

For three hours the actor was walked around the stage, sitting up, swinging his feet, swinging his arms, toying with his cap. Gradually the director and actor began to pick out elements. Instead of pulling back his shoulders, which were naturally stooped and sloped, they exaggerated the slope. They found a natural way of hooking his thumbs into his belt and exaggerated this action too. It also was found that keeping his hands in the back pockets was a natural habit of this actor, so this was also incorporated. Instead of talking out of the side of his mouth, he now opened his mouth wide and talked loudly and boisterously. One trait of his that didn't fit was his hesitant, drawly way of speaking. This would look almost incongruous with the rest of Curly. It was necessary for him to begin developing a faster rate of speech and completely eliminate the verbal "uh's." To help overcome this, he used his habit of toying with his cap and turned it into a clear-cut broad mannerism. He would rattle off a thought, shift his hat from one side to the other, then rattle off another thought. The character began to develop. As days went by, he added other mannerisms which helped to build up the character in mind.

A snag that developed was around the laugh, which was forced and artificial. Rather than retain an unconvincing laugh, the director decided to eliminate it entirely, even though this decision robbed Curly of some of his color. But one day, lying around, just musing and bantering back and forth, the actor happened, unconsciously, to strike on an unusual laugh, "whoa—whoa—whoa." Although preoccupied elsewhere, the director turned and pounced on this laugh with delight. The laugh became one of the charming highlights of the characterization.

The performance was enthusiastically received. Although there were large "holes" in the character, Curly was a great success. It was not a tough, bitter Curly. It was a jolly, cantankerous Curly. But it fitted well into the framework of the play. The character was unique, a creative job by a wise director.

With such an approach just described a bashful, withdrawn youngster could take the part of a boss, perhaps, but it would not be an aggressive, shouting boss. It might be a moody, distrustful, lonesome boss.

Artistic Success

It may seem to the reader that the matter of artistic success
is being unduly stressed.[17] It is true, of course, that success
in social growth is not measured in terms of the artistic
success of a performance but, rather, in the process leading
to the result—in the fulfillment of individual needs, in the
inculcation of desirable attitudes, in the enrichment of personality which are the by-products contained in this process.
But to say and recognize this is not to say we ignore the
results. Grace Coyle expresses it thus:

> . . . Success from the group worker's point of view is seen
> not in terms of games won, ceramics produced or information
> learned, but in terms of what the experience means to the
> participants. This does not mean a neglect of quality or accom-
> plishment. . . .[18]

Wilson and Ryland also comment as follows:

> . . . While a group is in session, the worker's first respon-
> sibility is to help the group-as-a-whole achieve its purposes. . . .
> It is in the process by which these purposes are achieved that
> the value of the group experience is rooted. The end is not
> so important as the means, yet the end is important. . . .[19]

> . . . End and means are interdependent; the end will have
> little significance if the means have failed to engage the inter-
> est and satisfy the needs of each member, and the means will
> have little sustained value if the end is disappointing. . . .[20]

There is more than one means to an end. We choose a
means, the creative approach, a process wherein is contained
the potential for bringing about better human relations. We
do not choose a mechanical approach with a set of external
techniques, a process which may well bring about the harmful
results to which Slavson has alerted us. But we must not
lose sight of the end. We must establish that artistic success
is possible through the creative approach. To ignore this end

or not, at least, to work for artistic success, whether it is achieved or not, would be a betrayal of the objectives of the participants. It becomes too easy, with such an attitude, to relax and not put in the required effort to accomplish the end which is the participant's goal. Let one member of the cast suspect that his director is not wholeheartedly working for artistic success but, rather, for what to him is some vague objective of developing his personality, and that person will begin to resent and mistrust such a director. The shy, withdrawn youngster playing the part of a boss must play this part with some feeling of successful accomplishment if the experience is to have positive value. He cannot play with success a shouting, aggressive boss if he is in no way a shouting, aggressive person. The result would be nothing more than superficial pretense.

Acting One's Self or Putting One's Self in Someone Else's Place

It has been believed by some that there is value in play participation because it allows the actor to put himself in someone else's place. Wilson and Ryland, for example, comment as follows:

The actor . . . is required to put himself into the experiences and feelings of someone else.[21]

There are always some who enjoy being the center of the stage . . . and need a great deal of help if they are to forget themselves and become the person in the play.[22]

Our young friend at the beginning of this chapter tells us after a hard experience, "You can never be anyone else even for a play." And in this he is joined by Stanislavski and his pupils. Stanislavski writes:

. . . Always and forever, when you are on the stage, you must play yourself. . . .
Never lose yourself on the stage. Always act in your own

person, as an artist. You can never get away from yourself. The moment you lose yourself on the stage marks the departure from truly living your part and the beginning of exaggerated false acting. Therefore, no matter how much you act, how many parts you take, you should never allow yourself any exception to the rule of using your own feelings. To break that rule is the equivalent of killing the person you are portraying, because you deprive him of a palpitating, living, human soul, which is the real source of life for a part.[23]

This concept of playing one's self is also recognized in the psychoanalytic field. Theodor Reik, for instance, in his famous book, *Listening with the Third Ear,* gives us a most interesting description of the process by which an actor might create the role of Hamlet. It will be noted that his analysis is quite in keeping with the Stanislavski method.

> . . . The greatest actors do not enter into the personality of a tragic hero, but they become Hamlet, so to speak. They do not imitate his experience, they actually experience his destiny, with the help of the same psychical possibilities within themselves, and of memory-traces of their own experience.
> . . . They do not enter into another's feelings, but unconsciously those feelings become their own. They are not resonance chambers for alien experience; but the resonance comes from the unconscious memory and revival of their own experience. Poetry has touched upon a fragment of buried inner life, has stirred the actor's own hidden possibilities. His acting is not the reproduction of an alien destiny, lived through in mimicry, but a possibility, unconsciously experienced in the past, of his own lot, which has found a point of contact with the other's. . . .[24]

If what Wilson and Ryland really mean is not so much to put one's self in someone else's feelings but rather in someone else's circumstances, then we would not be apart, for the emotion and temperament would still belong to the actor. This is a most important distinction, for in the former we are placed in the position of imagining how this character felt in a certain situation. Was he sad, elated, angry? Then we are led into the reproduction of some feeling of sadness, elatedness or anger, and from here we might as well go back to the list of such external techniques as listed in Crafton and Royer to determine how to express these emotions. We will then be led into the pitfall of forcing emotions, putting quivers in our voices, wringing our hands in anguish, all of which cannot help but be artificial and pretentious.

Professional Versus Amateur

The question arises, are we to expect, from what has so far been written, that our young amateurs are to become Marlon Brandos and Ernest Borgnines? After all, it will be said, an amateur theatre group is not a professional organization such as the Group Theatre. A social group worker once remarked to this writer that she really did not expect to enjoy an amateur performance, although, she hastened to add, it did not affect her acceptance of this medium as valuable in group work. When she wanted to enjoy a play as an aesthetic experience, she went to see a professional performance. She questioned whether there is not a distinction between amateur and professional drama.

To this writer it seems that such a distinction is one of degree, not of method or principle. For the purpose of a play is to produce an emotional effect upon the audience. Emotions do not distinguish between amateurs and professionals. Amateurs cannot address a plea to the audience's emotions to make allowances for their inexperience. The approach of an amateur group to the performance of a play must, therefore, be one in which the aim is to strive for artistic success.

We might speculate that an amateur actor should start with parts which most closely resemble his own experiences, which are close to his own cultural pattern, which deal with situations and conflicts of which the actor already has some understanding and sympathy. With more acting experience he may then expand to play roles dealing with circumstances more strange and unfamiliar.

Certainly the professional actor, like the professional ball player, needs intensive training not required by the amateur in order to be prepared for the arduous requirements of a career. The professional actor needs to develop his voice and his body so that they are pliable and adaptable to the variety of roles to which he may be assigned. He needs to develop mechanics, techniques, and a whole set of stage tricks to carry him over hundreds of performances, as against the amateur who gears himself for only a few. He may need to train himself in the arts of dancing, fencing, and singing.

As a matter of fact, many professional actors, Julie Harris, for example, reject the Stanislavski method of acting for professionals because of the fear that over the long haul they can lose control of themselves, go into hysterics, and find themselves doing things they never dreamed of doing.[25] Such an occurrence was made the theme of an old movie called "Double Life," in which Ronald Colman played the part of Othello and, after hundreds of performances during which he strived for near perfection, attained identification with the character to such a degree that he actually believed himself to be Othello and literally killed Desdemona on the stage.

If anything, the Stanislavski method is more suited to the amateur, who gives only one or two performances.

A pioneer in creative dramatics for children once suggested to this writer that if he wanted to work for personality development of the actor, he should use the form of creative dramatics, leaving the formal play as a medium for theatrical production. But with the use of the Stanislavski method, in the adapted form to be presented in the next few chapters, a creative social growth experience need not be denied the older adolescent and adult, an age group whose program needs have not been fully met in the recent preoccupation of interest in the young child and the aged. It is the author's speculation, too, that the really great actors who pour out their souls in their performances do use Stanislavski techniques, whether they admit it or not.

FOOTNOTES

1. James Tintner, "My First Play," 1947. By permission.

2. W. David Sievers, "Autopsy on 'The Group,'" *The Quarterly Journal of Speech,* December, 1949, p. 473.

3. Toby Cole, Compiler, *Acting: A Handbook of the Stanislavski Method* (New York: Crown Publishers, Inc., 1947, 1955), as found in the "Introduction" by Lee Strasberg, p. 16.

4. Allen Crafton and Jessica Royer, *The Complete Acted Play* (New York: Appleton-Century-Crofts, Inc., 1945), p. 151. By permission of the publisher.

5. *Ibid.,* p. 120.

6. *Ibid.,* p. 120.

7. From "The Work of the Actor" by I. Rapoport, included in *Acting: A Handbook of the Stanislavski Method* compiled by Toby Cole. Copyright 1947, 1955, by Crown Publishers, Inc. Used by permission of the publisher.

8. *See* Toby Cole, Compiler, *op. cit.,* as found in "Stanislavski's Method of Acting," by M. A. Chekhov, p. 106.

9. From "The Creative Process" by I. Sudakov, included in *Acting: A Handbook of the Stanislavski Method* compiled by Toby Cole. Copyright 1947, 1955, by Crown Publishers, Inc. Used by permission of the publisher.

10. Gordon Hamilton, *Theory and Practice of Social Case Work* (New York: Columbia University Press, 1940), pp. 194-195. By permission of the publisher.

11. Toby Cole, Compiler, *op. cit.,* as found in "The Work of the Actor" by I. Rapoport, pp. 34-37.

12. *Ibid.*

13. From "The Work of the Actor" by I. Rapoport, included in *Acting: A Handbook of the Stanislavski Method* compiled by Toby Cole. Copyright 1947, 1955, by Crown Publishers, Inc. Used by permission of the publisher.

14. The sections from *An Actor Prepares* by Constantin Stanislavski, translated by Elizabeth Reynolds Hapgood, are quoted by permission of its publisher, Theatre Arts Books, Copyright 1936 by Theatre Arts, Inc., Copyright 1948 by Elizabeth R. Hapgood.

15. Rudolph M. Wittenberg, *So You Want to Help People* (New York: Association Press, 1947), p. 47.

16. Gertrude Hartman and Ann Shumaker (editors for The Progressive Education Association), *Creative Expression* (Milwaukee: E. M. Hale and Company, 1939), p. 257.

17. It may be well to mention that all drama schools do not accept the Stanislavski method. Indeed, many schools do achieve considerable success with methods other than those mentioned here. The Drama Department of Catholic University of America in Washington, D.C., is an example of a theatre group highly regarded nationally which rejects, in the main, the Stanislavski point of view. This writer does not claim that the creative approach as described here is the only method of producing an artistic success of a play.

18. Grace L. Coyle, *Group Work with American Youth* (New York: Harper & Brothers, 1948), p. 28.

19. Gertrude Wilson and Gladys Ryland, *Social Group Work Practice* (Boston: Houghton Mifflin Company, 1949), p. 63.

20. *Ibid.,* p. 97.

21. Wilson and Ryland, *op. cit.,* p. 293.

22. *Ibid.,* p. 287.

23. See footnote 14 above.

24. From *Listening with the Third Ear,* copyright 1948 by Theodor Reik. By permission of Farrar, Straus and Cudahy, Inc., publishers.

25. *See* Seymour Peck, "The Temple of 'The Method,'" article in *The New York Times Magazine,* Section 6, Part I, May 6, 1956, p. 48.

CHAPTER THREE

How to Do It—The Beginning Stage

IN ORDER TO ILLUSTRATE how the creative approach can be applied, we would now like to take the reader through a step-by-step description of the writer's direction of a play. The particular selection was the classic, "A Christmas Carol," from the story by Charles Dickens, as adapted by Cora Wilson Greenwood. Presenting the play was the drama club of a small Lutheran religious and liberal arts college. Arrangements with the director of the drama club, an extracurricular activity at this school, had been made by the writer to direct this play.

Limitations were many. The writer had no previous contact with the cast or with the college. Time permitted only twelve rehearsals, far too few, particularly in using the creative approach. Most of the roles had already been cast; the actors to fill other roles were not found until a few days before the performance. But it still seems best here to use as an example an experience with many limitations, as more closely resembling reality situations than one with ideal conditions. The form of a diary will be followed in describing the process of bringing this play to life.

Rehearsal 1. Understanding the Play.

We read the play through to get a sense of the whole. Director (D) asks how cast likes the play. Scrooge (actors will be identified by the characters they are portraying) says he cannot play the part; he doesn't fit the character at all; his voice is way too high. Others agree, pointing to Lionel Barrymore as an opposite type.

D: What is the purpose of this play?
Scrooge: To bring the story to life.
D: What is the purpose of the story?
   (A pause—hesitation—finally . . .)
Girl (with a note of desperation and antagonism): To show Scrooge's greed . . .
D: Ah, yes! Well, now, then, is the characteristic of greed necessarily lodged in a voice that's raspy, growly, low, and coarse?

All look at each other and begin to smile. Scrooge grins broadly and says he will take the part.

Comments: The first step is the reading of the play. The first purpose is the clear understanding of the story. Before this the director should himself know the play thoroughly, place the climaxes, main and subordinate, formulate the theme and the main conflicts. In this rehearsal time ran out with the discussion of greed. Time permitting, we would have also included the retelling of the story in our own words, reconstructing the sequence of events.

Rehearsals 2 and 3. Studying the Characters.

Working for Naturalness.

Digging into Meanings.

Breaking Up Lines into Thoughts.

D begins by demonstrating the difference between reading and natural conversation through a diagram on the blackboard. In reading or reciting one usually speaks with an even-flowing rhythm with distinct pauses on the periods. In natural conversation the speech would be more jerky and animated, with a great variety in pace and in pitch, and with inflection according to the natural emphasis and stress of ideas which the meaning would bring forth spontaneously. Conversation thinks not of sentence units but of ideas to be made clear.

D demonstrates both manners of speech in the following example, given first as if read from a book or story and then as if related in everyday conversation between friends:

> I was standing on the corner of Seventh and Wabasha, waiting for a streetcar. I waited for a long time, but it didn't come. It was awfully cold. I went into the drugstore to warm up. I kept looking out of the window for what seemed hours. I got so mad I could have thrown something through the bay window.

D concludes that we must strive for animation and naturalness, so that the audience will get the feeling that this is the first time these thoughts have been spoken.

Then, with the cast seated on the stage, we start to read the play through again, stopping quite often to discuss the meanings of the lines. In this play the setting is introduced to the audience by means of a Reader. The rehearsal continues as follows:

READER: Once upon a time, of all good times in the year, on Christmas Eve, old Ebeneezer Scrooge, member of the firm of Scrooge, Marley & Company, sat busy in his countinghouse. It was cold, bleak, biting weather, and he could hear the people in the court outside go wheezing up and down, beating their hands upon their breasts and stamping their feet. . . .

Reader is singsong-y, emphasizing the words "Ebeneezer Scrooge."

D (interrupting): Has it been said that *someone else*, not Ebeneezer Scrooge, sat busy in his countinghouse?

READER: No.

D: Then why such a great emphasis on the words "Ebeneezer Scrooge"? (Reader frowns in puzzlement.) Tell me in your own words what the Reader is trying to say.

READER: That Ebeneezer Scrooge, on a certain day, *sat busy in his countinghouse.*

D: Right! We must learn to convey the thoughts and ideas we wish by emphasizing them properly, focusing on the main thoughts, knowing what is primary and what is subordinate. Okay, let's go on now.

READER (continuing): It was cold, bleak, biting . . .

D (interrupting and addressing everybody): Please repeat after me, "She was a tall, thin, angular woman." (They do.) Now, can you give me that line with imagery? By this I mean can you say it so that you have a picture of tallness, thinness and angularity in your mind? Can you say it so that it sounds like what it means?

A jumble of various interpretations issue forth. D demonstrates with his own.

D (to Reader): Now can you apply this same idea to the words "bold," "bleak," "biting," and so on?

Reader tries; it sounds better, but she is still reading rather than telling a story.

D: If you will use this idea of verbal imagery throughout your study of these lines, you won't have to worry about such things as enunciation. *See* what you are saying, get yourself interested and awed by it and *tell* it, don't read it. We shall not even consider you a Reader. We shall suppose that you're a mother telling this story to a child. In fact, we shall have children sitting in front of you for the performance.

Thus do we go on, stopping occasionally to analyze meanings of lines and talking about characters.

Now we are at the scene where the Collector asks Scrooge for a donation. After deciding that the Collector is a salesman, we come to the speech where Scrooge scathingly condemns Christmas.

D (interrupting the reading): Do you suppose Scrooge really hates the idea of Christmas as much as he says?

SCROOGE: No question about it. He is flatly opposed to Christmas.

GIRL (thoughtfully): No, I think he might have been so poor at one time that he can't face the idea of being poor again.

GHOST OF CHRISTMAS PAST: He is covering up his real feelings about Christmas.

SCROOGE: You're both way off the beam! (Discussion gets hot and heavy.)

D (interrupting): Let me summarize. There are three different points of view. They are all legitimate. Frankly, I like the idea that something is behind his apparent hatred of Christmas. Have you observed in everyday life that when people get overly angry about something, they usually are trying to cover up the fact that they're not too sure of themselves? People who are sure of themselves don't need to yell their convictions.

SCROOGE (still not convinced): I never get angry, so I wouldn't know.

D (giving him his rein): It's up to you what interpretation you want to use. It is important to fix on some definite interpretation, however, for that will determine your action on the stage. But I do want to emphasize that the only way the controversy can really be settled, both as to Scrooge's attitudes and the attitudes of all other characters, is to learn more about human behavior. Observe everyday life, for there lies the source of our material for acting.

We come to the scene of Marley's Ghost. A long discussion ensues about whether ghosts can be real. Marley insists that since ghosts are not human, we can't make him real. He wants to develop some kind of eerie tone for the ghost, pointing to stage directions in the book for support.

D: Since none of us have ever been ghosts, we have no way of determining their humanness. We can, therefore, use our own judgment and imagination and create him any way we like. Your interpretation is valid, but there is the danger that with an eerie monotonous tone, he may not get his meanings across. The ghost may not be human, but you certainly are. As a human being, *what would you do if you were a ghost?* You will have to do a lot of thinking about it. Use your imagination. See if you can visualize yourself with your own feelings in the position of a ghost. Will he or will he not be emotional?

Marley is not convinced. D tells him to try his own interpretation.

In the scene between Ghost of Christmas Past and Scrooge, D interrupts on Ghost's line: "Strange to have forgotten it so many years, strange. But let us go on."

D: Ghost, I have the feeling we're still reciting and reading and not really getting the meanings.

GHOST: How do you want me to say the line?

D (shrugging): How do you feel you should say it? Why is the Ghost telling this to Scrooge?

GHOST (persisting after some discussion of this): If you would just tell me how you want the line given, we wouldn't waste so much time.

D: I could easily give you *my* idea of how the line should be said, but then you would only be imitating me. Wouldn't you rather create your own? Here's the idea! (D searching around; he can't seem to find what he is after; acts perplexed.) "Now, *that's* funny. I could swear I put my briefcase here and now it's gone. That's *funny*." You see what I mean? The first "funny" is different from the second "funny." You've got to break your lines down into thoughts. "Strange to have forgotten it so long" is one thought. The second "strange" is a new thought. "But let us go on" is a third thought. Three thoughts in one line. Show us by something in your manner that you are making a transition from one thought to another—that you've been *struck* with the fact that it really is strange. Then show us that—well, it's

no use lingering on this—what's gone is gone—and continue
to your third thought, "Let us go on."
GHOST (dryly): I see.

As the rehearsal time draws to a close, D calls attention to
the danger of hoarseness, particularly in the case of Scrooge.
The cast is put through a voice exercise. In unison they draw
their arms back as if to pitch a baseball, they breathe deeply,
they throw the imaginary ball, saying "Ha" at the same time.

Scrooge remains after the rest of the cast has left. D walks
him around, relaxing him, looking for natural characteristics
which will fit well into the character. The actor is tall, wiry,
wrinkly. He has a wiggly hand gesture which we fasten upon
as a major gesture upon which he can always fall back. He
also has a peculiar mannerism of scratching his head, which
lends itself quite well too. Scrooge asks about age. D explains
this should come last in the process of creating the role. As he
gradually probes the meanings of the lines and begins to react
to others in a way which is logical to him, he will begin to
feel older and the age will, in a sense, creep on to the character. However, D does illustrate one aspect of age by asking
him to reach up as if to grab an apple, first as a child, then
an adult, and then an old man. Scrooge sees differences.

Comments: We work for a natural conversational quality
and for meanings of lines. Care must be taken not to belabor
points. The process of putting a play together is like the process of tightening the lugs on a wheel when repairing a tire.
One tightens all the lugs gradually. The first lug is tightened
part-way, then the next and the next. Then one goes through
the same process over and over again until all the lugs are
thoroughly and securely tightened. The steps in the production of a play require the same focus on the total. One should
not try to extract *all* the meanings nor determine *all* the
nuances of interpretation the first time around. The main objective is to plant seeds so that the cast's imagination will
blossom.

Resistance to D and disagreements within the cast are normal. In fact, they may be good indications that such seeds are taking root. In view of such resistance, note that D allows both Scrooge and Marley their own rein. Should D have engaged in a debate with either of them over the matter of interpretation, such argument would only have increased their resistance and raised further objections. The final creation and resolution of the character, if it is to come from the heart and soul of the actor, must come about as a result of his own thinking. It is only in this way that social growth can be obtained.

In this instance, from reports received, the resistance was more on a personal basis. There was an undercurrent of resentment toward D who, it seemed to the cast, was an intruder.

The concept of verbal imagery and the technique of paraphrasing are used by D continually throughout all the rehearsals. D did not tell Ghost how to say the line because such a procedure would have been out of line with the creative approach. Telling an actor how to say his line would accomplish at best an imitation of the director. Moreover, the director may give the line for him but not do it quite right. The actor then would imitate the director's version of the line, again having it not quite right. This could only result in artificiality. Effective use of paraphrasing requires a great deal of imagination on the part of a would-be director.

Rehearsals 4 and 5. Associating Meanings with Movement (Blocking).

Now the cast gets on its feet. The play is broken down into individual scenes. The following procedure is used: The cast, still with scripts in hand, goes through the scene, using any action deemed fit, with no interruptions from D. Then the scene is gone through again, almost line by line. We fix specifically the places on stage and the particular movement that goes with the lines, using the actor's own action as a basis, but modifying as is necessary to keep the characters from blocking each other out of sight. Emphasis is always on the actor's comfort and feeling of naturalness. Then the scene is gone through as a whole once more.

Throughout there is continual stress on motivation, the reason that the character behaves as he does. For example: In the first scene, Bob Cratchit asks Scrooge for the day off on Christmas Day. Scrooge delivers a diatribe against Christmas, Cratchit turning around to listen to him. When Scrooge finishes his blast, Cratchit again asks for the day off. Scrooge reluctantly grants it.

D: What about this fellow Cratchit? Is he to be cringing, bowing, scraping before this Scrooge? Is he going to let him get away with a blasphemous speech like that? What does he think of Scrooge, anyway?

CRATCHIT: I think he kind of likes the old buzzard even with all his grouchiness. He lets those things wash off.

D: You mean he's heard Scrooge say these things before and it isn't as bad as it sounds?

CRATCHIT: He's probably been working for him for a long time and is used to it. He might have seen better days under him. At least he still feels sort of loyal to him.

D: But isn't it possible, too, that he's just plain afraid of him— not physically, but simply because he might lose his job and jobs might be scarce?

CRATCHIT: I don't think that's it so much as he is just pretty used to him. At the end of the play, remember, he is glad to see Scrooge and invites him to dinner.

D: All right, then. Your interpretation is quite valid. You must make us see, then, what your attitude is. You have decided you would rather be resigned than be humble and crawling. Why turn around and look at him, then, when he's blasting away at Christmas? Why not just stand there with your back toward him, as if to say, "There he goes, blowing his top again. I'll just sit this one out." If you do this, you are

giving a motivation for standing there with your back toward him. How you motivate every action of yours is what
constitutes good, creative acting.

We try this out and Cratchit agrees he feels much more
natural this way. Therefore, we fix this position and movement in relation to the motivation decided upon.

We follow the same procedure with the Collector and
Scrooge. The Collector goes through quite a few changes in
mood—from hopeful optimism, to bewilderment, to anger
and, finally, to disgust.

In this scene a rather long argument ensues between the
Collector and Scrooge. Scrooge has been sitting at a table all
this time. D points out that it is too long a time for one
position to be maintained; drama needs variety. We experiment until we find the most effective line upon which Scrooge
can get up from his chair and move to a different position
on the stage. This line comes after a long speech by Collector explaining the plight of the poor.

COLLECTOR (at the end of speech): "What shall I put you down
    for?"
SCROOGE: "Nothing!"
COLLECTOR: "You wish to be anonymous?"
SCROOGE: "I wish to be left alone . . ."

This is the line upon which Scrooge gets up from the chair
and moves to the other side of the stage. The argument has
worn on Scrooge and he is becoming genuinely irritated.
Scrooge's first try is awkward. D demonstrates, paraphrasing:

D: My God, man. How many times do I have to tell you? No!
    Can't you understand that? No!

Scrooge's next try is much improved. Now his movement
is motivated by a burst of emotion, a sudden impatience with
the way the argument is going. This line becomes the climax
of this scene.

We turn now to the rest of the speech, "I don't make merry myself at Christmas—my partner, Marley, never did—and I can't afford to make idle people merry . . ." and so on, attempting to justify his refusal of a donation.

D: Is Scrooge attempting to justify his action to the Collector or to himself? (A pause.) After all, what does he care about the Collector? He may never see him again anyway. Besides, Scrooge doesn't appear to be the sort of person who is concerned about what others think of him.

GIRL: Personally, I don't care what others think of me. If I'm sure I'm right, the whole world can go fly a kite. I think Scrooge is really worried over what he thinks of himself.

D: Ah, what he thinks of himself . . . that is important.

We arrive at a movement, then, in which Scrooge paces up and down agitated, not paying any attention to the Collector. His rationalization is delivered almost to the walls, as if trying to convince himself he is justified.

Collector's next line, "Many would rather die than go there," turns Scrooge back to the Collector. Now Scrooge answers directly and definitely: "If they would rather die— they had better do it and decrease the surplus population." A slight pause, and then with the next line, "Besides, that's not my business . . . ," Scrooge returns to the table, indicating the interview is closed—period. (During the final performance the Collector's final "good night" was a little highlight. These two words were so uniquely expressed that they conveyed his whole attitude, as if to say, "For Pete's sake, let me out of here. This guy's crazy!") During the rest period that follows, Cratchit tells D it is a real education to watch this type of direction.

Up to this point, D has discouraged the learning of lines as such. His emphasis has been on the understanding of the play as a whole and on the study of the meanings of lines. Now he asks that the actors begin to learn lines inasmuch as they have movements and positions with which to associate them.

Comments: The step here described is that of blocking out. People in real life naturally group themselves so as not to obstruct anyone from view. This is also done on the stage with the added thought in mind of throwing the focus of attention on whatever or whomever the requirements of the play would dictate. This writer believes that the blocking, after a period of experimentation, should be fixed specifically, so that the actor knows the exact line on which he is to rise, sit, or walk, and the exact position where he is to be. There are those creative enthusiasts who might claim that such rigid fixing will inhibit creativity on the part of the actor. By leaving movements to chance, however, there is too much danger of creating unnecessary tensions on the part of the others on the stage. Confronted with unexpected movements, an actor, especially an amateur, could become flustered and allow his attention to be diverted from his role. Specific blocking, on the other hand, will give a certain security to the cast as a whole. Much of the socializing value of drama would be lost were actors to be given the complete freedom to run around the stage in any way they felt at a given moment. Within the framework of specific blocking, there is ample opportunity for creativity.

The idea of fixing the blocking specifically is a departure from the pure Stanislavski method which permits a great deal of spontaneous improvisation. We point out again, however, that our method of direction is a modification and adaptation of the pure Stanislavski method to fit our own needs and conditions. Stanislavski himself urged adaptation and change. In speaking with Joshua Logan and Charles Leatherbee who were studying the Moscow Art Theatre's methods, he advised:

> You must not duplicate the Moscow Art Theatre in America. You must create something of your own. . . . If something excites you, apply it to yourselves, but adapt it. . . . Let it make you think further.[1]

The reader will note that this is the first time there has been any mention of learning lines. It takes some patience to hold off this long but the director's seeming unconcern, at the beginning, with memorization of lines helps focus attention on the meaning of lines and the understanding of the play. It helps assure that when lines are learned they will not be the result of rote memory. It is also easier to learn lines when there are movements and meanings with which to associate them.

With more time, this phase of rehearsal could very well begin with some exercise such as suggested by Lee Strasberg, a former director of the Group Theatre of New York, and now director of the Actor's Studio in New York:

> With the cast all seated ask one to walk around—no reasons given. Then ask him to walk around a second time, now thinking about the latest movies he has seen. (Check to see if he actually carries this out.) The difference between the two walks should be enlightening.[2]

It can readily be seen how, with more time, much more could be done in the way of exploring motivations and mechanisms. Under the stress of time, D often becomes more of an explainer than the provocateur he would prefer to be, drawing the interpretations out of the cast.

Rehearsal 6. Blending and Refining Meanings and Motivations with Movements and Characterization

                  Taking Scenes Apart and Putting them Together.

We are still discussing the characterization of the ghosts.

D: The purpose of the play is to produce an emotional effect on the audience.

SCROOGE (facetiously): Except for the playwright, it's a way of making money.

D: How do we produce an emotional effect?

GIRL: By making the play real.

GHOST: By feeling it ourselves.

D: Good. Now we are talking about whether ghosts can be emotional. What is the ghost trying to do?

GHOST: To get Scrooge to change his ways.

D: How?

GHOST: By being cold and indifferent.

GIRL: By treating him the same way he has treated others.

SCROOGE: By being cold and unsympathetic.

GHOST: By being angry.

D: Not indifferent? If we want to make him angry, then he must be alive with expression. Perhaps it might be possible to portray indifference through eerie monotones. But why take chances? Especially as amateurs, we need at least sufficient variety to get meanings across.

We run through the scene between Scrooge and the Ghost of Christmas Present, the third ghost to appear.

D: How does Scrooge feel differently here?

GHOST: He is very much softened.

GIRL: He is willing to take the visit of the next ghost.

SCROOGE: He is still afraid, but he wants more of the lesson the ghosts are teaching him.

D: He has already been through a terrific experience. He has already exerted a great emotional effort. Wouldn't it be the same as if he just came out of a tough football game?

SCROOGE: In other words, all done in.

D: Right. Practically resigned.

SCROOGE: I shouldn't show much force then. Is it due to physical exhaustion?

D: Have you ever argued with someone for three hours and never gotten anywhere?

SCROOGE: I have never proposed to a girl . . .

D: Have you ever argued about religion?

SCROOGE: Yes, and lost.

READER: You shouldn't give up something you believe in.

SCROOGE: I didn't—but I lost.

READER (smugly): But in religion you don't lose unless you give up.

We run through the scene again.

D: Don't sit down, Scrooge, until the Ghost talks to you. Have movements motivated.

SCROOGE: Does that rule always hold?

D: Nothing *always* holds.

Scene between Girl and Young Scrooge:

D: What, in your own words, is the Girl trying to tell Young Scrooge?

GIRL: That he is putting wealth above everything in life, and that she would be secondary to wealth.

D: She is doing this for her own protection?

YOUNG SCROOGE: Yes.

D: Then why is she leaving him? What has happened? Did Young Scrooge propose? Are they engaged?

YOUNG SCROOGE: I proposed while I was still poor.

D: Why doesn't Young Scrooge act anything but downcast? What is his real attitude? (A blank pause.) If he feels sure that the Girl comes first, his whole action would be different than it would if he really knows that there is something in what she says. (The cast is still puzzled.) What is the Girl objecting to?

GIRL: Just in general—his attitude has changed.

D: How?

GIRL: A gradual process of getting more and more interested in wealth.

D: How is his attitude expressed?

GIRL: In not caring about the idealistic things any more.

SCROOGE: In caring about hard cash.

D: But hasn't he done something?

GIRL: I hadn't thought about it.

D: How do we determine people's attitudes?

SOMEONE: By their actions, of course.

GIRL: But an attitude like that to a person who knows another real well would be obvious without actions. I could find out by talking to him. His whole philosophy would be changed.

D: What was his philosophy once?

GIRL: More idealistic, "noble aspirations," he wanted to help mankind.

D: And now?

GIRL: Now he wants to make and keep money.

D: Have you known people like that who have changed in attitude? You know, idealistic attitudes are likely to change to more realistic ones. What do they say about young college radicals? It's okay if they're radical in college; they'll all be conservative by the time they're thirty . . .

COLLECTOR: I wouldn't know—I'm still in college, so I'm still idealistic.

D: There must be something he did . . . what is the precipitating factor here that made the Girl change toward Young Scrooge, that made her suddenly indignant?

COLLECTOR: But true love never changes. She couldn't have loved him. If it was really love, it could never have changed.

D (persisting): But there was one certain thing that must have happened to have brought this issue to a head. Some one thing, one final culmination in the eyes of the Girl of all she has been building up inside herself toward him. What could be that one thing that would be the last straw?

SCROOGE (triumphantly): She wanted to hear the Messiah on Christmas Eve, and I wanted to work!

GIRL: That does it! That would make me furious!

Comments: D does not accept ideas in general. He presses for the concrete evidence of attitudes and events. He tries to get actors to imagine vividly the specific events which will produce the emotion.

Rehearsal 7. The Actor as a Whole.

Acting and Reacting

Blending In of Lines.

We carry on as before, taking separate scenes and working them through for motivation, for characterization, and for extracting still more meaning from lines. Then we take the scene as a whole, with no interruptions. With a few exceptions, notably Scrooge, all are still reading from the script. D places great emphasis now on learning of lines. He begins to insist that the actors give their lines without the script in the best way they can, so as to blend them in with the action and the movement—so that the acting gets into their muscles, as it were.

D calls attention to an awkward position of Scrooge, who, after making a cross (walking from one part of the stage to another), ends up sort of suspended on tiptoe. D explains the concept of empathy, demonstrating. If we don't move as a whole, if we don't react as a total, we end up with something like the uncomfortable position of Scrooge, or with a twisting of the neck. Our actions on the stage are vicariously imitated by the audience, very much like the passenger in a car who vicariously imitates the driver when he presses down on the brake.

Cratchit interrupts to call attention to an article in *Life* magazine, showing a movie audience puckering up their lips as they watch a kissing scene.

D: That's exactly the idea. The audience can get a pleasant empathy or an unpleasant empathy from our actions on the stage. When you turn, turn definitely, clearly—not just your head or neck, for this gives the audience a bad empathy. If Scrooge walks, he should walk with his whole self, not just his feet. He should know where he is going and go there definitely and clearly, not haphazardly and uncertainly, unless he wants to convey uncertainty. But then he should be certain about his uncertainty.

Finally, it is established to Marley's satisfaction that a portrayal of the ghost as human would be rational and effective. We settle on Marley's ghost being emotional and suffering, Ghost of Christmas Past to be ominous and foreboding,

Ghost of Christmas Present to be, on the one hand, jolly and cheerful and, on the other, sarcastic and angry.

Comments: Empathy here is used in a more restricted sense than it is in social work. It is useful in that it can point up defects in physical action.

FOOTNOTES

1. Constantin Stanislavski, *Building a Character* (New York: Theatre Arts Books, Robert M. MacGregor, 1949), pp. xiv-xv.

2. John Gassner, *Producing the Play* (New York: The Dryden Press, 1941); Lee Strasberg, "Acting and the Training of the Actor," pp. 141-142.

CHAPTER FOUR

How to Do It—The Finishing Stage

THERE COMES A TIME during rehearsals when the director must decide to begin working toward "getting the show on the road," as it were. He cannot wait for the fullest exhaustion of all the learning possibilities. He must accept what he has and begin to go about the business of integrating it all into a total. From here on there will be less discussion and more overt direction. We continue with our diary of rehearsals.

Rehearsal 8. The Play as a Total.

D was getting concerned about the failure to have had, as yet, a complete run-through of the whole play. It is not possible yet, however, for there are some absences. A person to play the part of the character of Fred, Scrooge's nephew, has not yet been found. Moreover, today is the first appearance of Mrs. Cratchit.

The scene where Mr. and Mrs. Cratchit look at Tiny Tim, lying dead on a cot, has not yet been touched. D simply creates a series of movements for Mrs. Cratchit to follow in co-ordination with her lines. There is no time for probing now. We must have the play set so that a run-through can be obtained.

Cratchit complains that this scene is too mushy and sentimental. He doesn't see how he can do it. D suggests an interpretation somewhat different from that indicated in the book. On the line "My little Tim! My little Tim!" instead of breaking down with sobs, he might just look at Tim, contemplating the tragedy, remembering Tim as he was, playing in the yard or fidgeting at the table. On the second "My little Tim" he could walk away from him, as if to say, "It's certainly too bad." Cratchit seemed almost grateful for this interpretation, but he never could quite be heard in this one scene, even during the performance. He somehow couldn't get himself sold on the validity of the situation.

Comments: Imposing an interpretation should, of course, be avoided if at all possible. At least it does serve to point up that external techniques by themselves cannot produce the sincerity of the emotion or the situation. What could have been done much earlier in rehearsals was to have helped Cratchit recall for himself previous experiences of tragedy and how he as a person reacted. At this point in the production of the play, however, it was almost impossible to avoid some expedient manipulation and a handed-down interpretation because of the limitation of time and because of the urgency of clearing the way for a complete run-through. D knows from previous experience that the great hurdle is yet to come, for it is one thing to be able to repeat lines to oneself in the quiet of one's own bedroom and another thing to throw them out on a stage where they are part of the actor as a whole. Thus the vital necessity to have a complete run-through as soon as possible.

Rehearsal 9. Working for Sincerity of Feeling.

We finally get started on the last phase, running through the whole play. This is followed by criticism by D and selection of scenes and individuals needing special attention. Though lines are not yet learned, scripts are put away. The cast is not to stop for anything; prompting will be done from the audience the first few times, but if it is not forthcoming, the actors are to stay in character and carry on somehow.

Criticism by D consists now of challenges to their sincerity of portrayal, provoking more genuineness of expression. D's running expression is "You need to *convince* me." He is careful also to point to spots in which they *do* achieve genuine feeling, using these as examples of how other scenes can be improved.

The run-through is disjointed and confused. Scrooge, Collector, and Marley carry on ad-libs like hardened veterans but they break into laughs. D keeps insisting that the play go on. Ghost of Christmas Past forgets a line and stops completely.

D: Don't break; keep on going.

But Ghost turns to audience and asks a question. D promptly asks that the scene be started from the beginning again. He insists that it is vital at this point to get acclimated to meeting unexpected obstacles and to go on as if nothing had happened. There will be no prompting on the night of performance. Any little stop informs the audience that something is wrong, that they have forgotten a line, and breaks the magic of the play.

Comments: D feels quite discouraged. Nothing seems to have gone right. He cannot see how the play could possibly come off in less than a week. But he recalls previous experiences where the same process has taken place. There always have been retrogressions, particularly when cast members have not yet accustomed themselves to rehearsing without the scripts.

At this point D's role is changing from that of a teacher and helper to that of a full-fledged director, giving orders, insisting that certain commitments be carried out. There may be certain resistances, but the group as a whole is ready to accept D in this role, for they too are beginning to become apprehensive about the success of the performance. Now they welcome a co-ordinator—a task which, by its nature, necessarily belongs to the director. Knowing that this responsibility is acknowledged and accepted by D is a source of security to the cast.

Rehearsals 10 and 11. The Teamwork.

Polishing.

Dramatic Climaxes.

More run-throughs, criticism by D following. Criticism includes calling attention to needed transitions from one thought to another, pointing out good and poor reactions to each other. D stresses the ensemble work—listening to each other, watching each other.

D calls attention to some small gesture or mannerism that should be used or eliminated. Scrooge, for example, for the first time pointed at his chin with his forefinger. This is good and he is told to use it. Attention is also called to key words that are missed or to certain words on which the wrong emphasis has been placed.

D (to Reader): A *what* cell?
READER: A *cold, dismal* cell.

The weakest part of the run-through is the reading between the scenes. D has failed almost completely to help Reader, who has attended rehearsals faithfully, even when once ordered by her doctor to her bed. She is still singsong-y, affected, using a false dreaminess in her tone with the result that few of the meanings were actually coming across. D has concentrated so much on what was taking place on stage all this time that he has neglected to watch the reading taking place off stage between scenes. He now spends some time individually with Reader. She is relaxing too much, leaning back, kicking one shoe off and on. D tries to place her in a position in which she is forced to bend forward with her two feet solid on the floor. He points out her word-for-word pattern, giving to words like "to" and "of its" the same importance as "cell" and "busy." D makes the mistake of pointing out that even in singing it is the thoughts that are sung, not words. But Reader is a music major and argues back that it is the vowels that are stressed in music. The controversy is not resolved. Reader is defensive and unresponsive. However, she does make a slight improvement.

This is the first appearance of Fred, Scrooge's nephew. This actor appears somewhat effeminate. On the stage he is a swayer, delivering a line, then swaying back and forth until it is time for his next line. D gives him many movements to dissipate the nervous energy. D asks him what he ordinarily does with his hands.

FRED: Keep them in my pocket, I guess.
D: Fine! Keep them in your pocket. But don't let me think they're there just to keep them out of the way. Do something definite with them. Gesture with them in your pocket. Let the audience think that you're proud to have hands in pockets—that anyone who doesn't like it can lump it. (D demonstrates. Fred smiles, puzzled but willing.)

Another weakness is the characterization of Young Scrooge. D tells him flatly, during criticism, that D simply cannot get a picture of anything from him. He comes across completely blank. All he does is go through the motions. D asks what is wrong. Does he understand all the meanings?

Young Scrooge explains that his idea is that he is unimpressed and that he is reacting that way. D shrugs. D is only the audience and, as such, can report only what actually registers on him. If Young Scrooge wants to interpret the role as a reaction of unimpressiveness, then he must show this positively, not blankly. It is perfectly all right with D if he interprets the character as a person who is unapproachable, just so he makes it clear.

The scene now is between Scrooge and the Ghost of Christmas Present. Ghost is having some difficulty with the following:

SCROOGE: ". . . Oh, no, kind Spirit, say he [Tim] will live and be spared."

GHOST: "Why so, if he be like to die, he had better do it and (*pointedly*) decrease the surplus population. Man—if man you be in heart—will you decide what man shall live, what man shall die? . . ."

At the beginning of this section Scrooge and Ghost are facing each other ("profile" in drama terminology). After Scrooge's plea, D suggests that Ghost turn and walk away from him flippantly and sarcastically on the lines "Why so," ending with "decrease the surplus population," at which Ghost comes to a complete halt and pauses while she thinks about the real significance of such a thought. Suddenly, on the lines "Man, if man you be," she turns on Scrooge with fury and anger—a complete change in mood, a build-up to a climax.

Ghost has difficulty with the pause. D keeps ad-libbing various things she might be thinking about during the pause. D explains that the pause and the things she is thinking about must provide her with the impulse to turn on Scrooge with anger.

Finally she strikes the right note. It was a real, genuine display of emotion which stopped all the whispering, mumbling, and studying by the rest of the cast. The Ghost walked up to D delightedly, almost awed.

GHOST: I was really mad!
SCROOGE: She certainly was. I could feel it myself!

Comments: D's negative criticism of Young Scrooge was deliberate and calculated. From reports received from the co-director, who was also Young Scrooge's speech teacher, he had taken the part with the attitude that it was really too small for him to bother with. Criticism was given in the manner described in order to produce anxiety. Up to this time Young Scrooge had been quite passive and indifferent. However, the criticism was not offered in a condemning or ridiculing manner. It was an objective, honest report of what impression was made on D as a trial audience, and it resulted in stimulating Young Scrooge to make something of his part.

D's role develops here also into that of a trial audience, reporting back the impressions made. It is often found advisable at this time to call in a friend or critic who can present a fresh viewpoint.

This phase is sometimes called polishing.[1]

It may be thought because of the emphasis given to internal techniques in this manuscript that external techniques are not employed at all. That this is by no means true can be seen in the scene between Scrooge and the Ghost of Christmas Past. The suggested walk and turn of the Ghost, an external technique, provided the spark that finally unlocked the chain of her inhibitions. But such a technique was used only together with the feelings and thoughts which motivated the turn. A would-be director should develop the facility of picturing movements to fit thoughts. He also needs a sense of focus on the significant points of the play so that he can create a build-up to a climax.

Rehearsal 12. Clinching the Play as a Total.

Ad-lib run-through. This is our last practice before the dress rehearsal. Criticism is waived in order to have another run-through completely in our own words. Reader is absent. D takes her part in order to demonstrate and give the play a start.

D (as Reader): Say, listen, boy! Have I got a story to tell you!
You know, there was once a guy named Scrooge, Ebeneezer
Scrooge. Was he a tightwad! You know what he does? Well,
here it is Christmas Eve, and he's sitting around counting
his money! He had a fellow who worked for him, name of
Cratchit. So Cratchit comes in to old Scrooge's office.

Cratchit and Scrooge fall right into the spirit of things,
carrying on with their own ad-libbing.

CRATCHIT: Say, Mr. Scrooge, I was wondering whether I could
have tomorrow off. You know, it's Christmas Day and the
kid is sick.

SCROOGE: What! A day off! What do you think I'm paying you
for? Get back to work!

The session becomes riotously funny. Everyone is laughing, including D.

COLLECTOR: How do you do, Mr. Scrooge? The reason I'm calling on you is that a bunch of us got together and thought
we'd take up a collection for the poor, you know, being it's
Christmas and all . . .

SCROOGE: Not interested! Go peddle your fish somewhere else!

COLLECTOR: But Mr. Scrooge! This is Christmas!

SCROOGE: Christmas, bah! (Pacing up and down.) It's nothing
but a bunch of commercialism anyway.

COLLECTOR: Ah, crumps! Some of these people are starving!
Poorhouses and prisons don't help. The least we can do is
give 'em a little cheer and comfort.

Scrooge breaks the sequence of the play, whips out his bill-
fold, turns to the audience, shrugging, "I can't help it," and
hands Collector two dollars, sending everyone into further
gales of laughter. But, for the most part, the ad-lib session
carries on through the entire play.

D notices that Fred has a habit of counting-on-the-fingers
and suggests heartily that this is good to use in emphasizing
each adjective in the following speech, ". . . It's brought me
a good time! A kind, forgiving, charitable, happy time."

Comments: The ad-lib session is a most valuable technique in play production. It gives the actors a sense of the play as a whole. It trains them to think in terms of what the actor would do if he were the character in that situation. It prepares him to think on his feet so that he can always carry on with the play, whether he happens to forget a line or not, and he learns that what is important is the whole play rather than letter-perfect, memorized lines. In the case of Fred, for example, who never did get his lines right during the dress rehearsals and the final performances, it proved a boon, for he kept right on going in his own words. The play did not stop, and the audience had no idea that lines were forgotten.

By using his own words the actor also begins to appreciate the better-thought-through and selected words of the author. Many vague meanings come to the surface and are threshed out. Many new spontaneous occurrences, movements, and gestures are revealed, which the director can seize upon and incorporate into characterizations.

Last but not least, the ad-lib rehearsal is a great tension reliever at a time when nerves are frayed and tempers shortened. A stronger bond is created in the group because they are really working together under challenging conditions.

There is danger, however, in having such an ad-lib session come as late as it did here, for humorous associations can be created which might give the actor a "set" during the performance and might interfere with his absorption in the play. Such a rehearsal should preferably take place at a time when the actor has just completed learning his lines.

The ad-lib run-through should not be used in such plays as "Golden Boy," to be presented in the next chapter because the language in such a play is already too close to the actor's own vocabulary. This type of exercise is mainly valuable when a play contains a great deal of unfamiliar words and unusual phraseology.

Dress Rehearsal

An expert has been called in for make-up and costumes. Children from a Receiving Home are brought in to play the children's parts and to form a small audience for the Reader. The rehearsal is treated as a regular performance.

The play runs smoothly. It does not stop once. Marley, in particular, reached a peak in creativity, displaying genuine emotion and feeling which gripped the small audience. Marley was very much pleased. During the criticism, afterward, he tells D that it certainly was much better having a human ghost.

It should also be mentioned that one of the children, a twelve-year-old girl, told Tiny Tim he was "real cute." Tiny Tim was played by a lone six-year-old in the Home, who had been a scapegoat for the other children. This particular girl who was now praising him was accustomed to pushing and kicking him out of her way in the Home.

Performances

D's role is confined to a brief talk to the cast before the play, emphasizing that the performance should be considered as another rehearsal. He watches the play out front. With this group D wants the cast to have the feeling that this is their show and that D's job is done. He feels they will be more relaxed, more secure in the demonstration of confidence in them that D shows by watching the play in the audience. This is not, however, a hard-and-fast rule.

Performances are smooth, with no stops or awkward pauses, and for the most part, the attention of the audience is held. In places there is surprise at the sincerity of emotion.

Evaluation

1. *Artistic Success of the Play as a Whole*. As a whole, the play was enthusiastically received by the audience. There

seemed to be particular appreciation of the sincerity of feeling and the naturalness of the playing. There was a gap between scenes in which the Reader failed to hold the attention of the audience. There were also weaknesses in scenes between Girl and Young Scrooge, as well as in one of the Cratchit family scenes. The weaknesses, however, were not serious enough to cause a clear-cut break in the movement of the play as a whole.

One of the classes at the college was given an assignment to turn in anonymous reviews of the play. There were no unfavorable comments as far as the enjoyment of the play as a whole was concerned. Indeed, there was a great deal of enthusiasm and surprise expressed at the quality of the performance.

2. *The Unique Characterization of Scrooge*. Because of the widespread acquaintanceship of the public with the Lionel Barrymore portrayal of Scrooge, our Scrooge in this rendition illustrates by contrast the uniqueness of characterization that can be achieved with the creative approach. Scrooge emerged as an alive, human being with conflicts about his greed. Even in his outward appearance he was unlike the stereotype of Scrooge. His voice was high and barking rather than raspy and growly. He was spry and active rather than bent and wobbly. He was cantankerous and mischievous rather than sly and calculating. He portrayed a sense of humor which delighted the audience. Most important, he was revealed as a man who already had planted within him the seeds of goodness, an interpretation in which Scrooge (the actor) agreed only after a long period of groping and thinking.

Such a characterization was achieved and, this writer is convinced, could only be achieved *through the creative approach*. Its real value in uncovering potentials was most vividly illustrated in the fact that perhaps the most moving scene in the play was that in which Scrooge wakes up from his dream and finds that he is alive. This was created almost in total by Scrooge himself, without any help from the director. The director's best contribution here was, in fact, his noninterference, his letting Scrooge alone, in encouraging him to do what he himself was doing spontaneously. It is certainly questionable whether such a creation could have come about without all the preliminary work of the director in the previous scenes as shown in the diary here. At this point in the play there could be no mistaking the audience's feeling of being as one with Scrooge, delighted with him in his rebirth. It was one of those rare moments in drama and in real life when it seems that the best there is in human beings is fused in a perfect state of harmony. And written all over the face of Scrooge, the actor, after the performance was the glow of satisfaction and the thrill of creativity in which one feels "This I and I alone did."

3. *Relationship Between Director and Cast.* In the field of human relations the relationship between the individuals as well as the director is as much an area of evaluation as is the successful consummation of the project itself. Were a play to result in artistic success at the cost of bad relationships, the project as a whole could not be considered successful.

As stated at the beginning of this illustration, the director had no previous acquaintance with the cast. By performance time, however, the cast as a whole had accepted the director. Marley stated it rather well in a reply to the director who remarked that he hadn't done anything for the cast which they could not have done for themselves. Marley said, "Oh, no, only the difference between what we were at the beginning and what we were at the end—that's all you did." Director did not insist on his own interpretations. Scrooge and Marley, particularly, who were argumentative at the beginning, made up their own minds and began to appreciate the director more and more.

4. *Success of the Experience to the Individual Partici-*

pants. Like Scrooge, Marley and the Ghost-of-Christmas-Present certainly had emotional release which was observable. Their beaming countenances bespoke their feeling of a job well done and an inner satisfaction which would be long lasting. To a somewhat lesser degree the Collector, who, like Young Scrooge, was brought into the play by pressure, became quite interested and basked in the general feeling of satisfaction. He stayed through many rehearsals which did not require his presence and participated in the discussions. Cratchit too seemed to enjoy the creative process.

Some failures, however, must also be pointed out. It is difficult to see how this experience could have meant much to Mrs. Cratchit. She was brought in a few days before the performances. She was not really interested; her attitude was one of doing the cast a favor. The director, for the sake of the rest of the cast, moved her around the stage like a pawn in a chess game.

Young Scrooge, as mentioned before, thought his part was too small to merit his serious consideration. Though he improved slightly, there was certainly lacking in his manner, after the show was over, that glow of satisfaction that seemed to emanate from most of the rest of the cast.

There seemed to be an interesting correlation between those who worked diligently, who achieved artistic success, and who also gained a feeling of successful accomplishment. The one exception here would be, perhaps, the Reader, who did invest a great deal of effort. She could not seem to rid herself of the tendency to "etherealize" her reading, blocked off all attempts on the part of the director to stir her imagination, held fast to her defenses. As a result, since she did not really seem to understand what she was reading, the experience, in our opinion, could not have held too much meaning for her.

Reading, of course, is an art in its own right and requires

a special skill of its own. Charles Laughton has made a new career for himself out of this art.

In these chapters we have focused on the how-to-do-it aspects of creative play production, on the techniques of eliciting from the actors their own unique portrayals of the characters and their own ideas. Whereas in these chapters the writer had no acquaintance and no relationship with the cast prior to the first rehearsal, in the illustration to follow he had, in contrast, a close relationship to each participant, as well as an intimate knowledge of each individual's background. In the following chapters, therefore, we shall be able to illustrate and focus much more on the meaningfulness of such an experience to the individual who participates in a play creatively directed.

FOOTNOTE

1. *See* John Dolman, Jr., *The Art of Play Production* (New York: Harper & Brothers, 1946), pp. 194-215. It lists many aspects which a director would want to check in the final stages of the process of production.

CHAPTER FIVE

The Use of Play Production
in a Residential Treatment Center

ON A HOT SUMMER NIGHT in 1954 a group of adolescents, thirteen to seventeen years of age, presented the play, "Golden Boy," by Clifford Odets, before a hushed, surprised audience of two hundred and fifty adults and children in the gymnasium-auditorium of a nationally known treatment center. Despite the poor acoustics in this high-ceilinged hall, the audience hung on every word. Group-living counselors, who were standing by fully expecting to be called upon to remove hyperactive, restless youngsters from the audience, found to their amazement that the children as well as the adults were glued to their seats, fully absorbed in the play.

If one realizes that five weeks of strenuous rehearsals had taken place in preparation for the performance, one can understand the extreme caution with which the clinical team of the institution gave this project its sanction. Many a heated discussion had taken place between the director, superintendent, case work staff, psychologist and psychiatrist in airing the risks this project would entail. And why not? Any dramatic activity in the past which required more than four meetings on the part of a group of such disturbed adolescents had been much too taxing on the limited attention span and frustration tolerance of these children. The director, however, felt confident that the risk was warranted not only because of the benefits to be gained from the project as a group activity, but also because there was the possibility that the play might emerge as a stimulant to therapy. Nevertheless, it was a full two years from the time the idea was first conceived before it was felt that the optimum conditions existed to undertake this project with confidence on the part of the staff. Before it was agreed to engage in this experiment, scenes from the play were eliminated to cut down the playing time to one hour and fifteen minutes in order to further insure against the devastating effects of a possible failure.

Now, as the final curtain was being drawn, the superintendent stepped to the stage and quieted the ear-splitting applause that greeted the youthful actors on the curtain call. With deep emotion he acclaimed the performance just witnessed as the highest point of recreational achievement in his ten years at the institution. His countenance beamed with pride as he lauded the cast members for their abundance of faith and confidence and their perseverance in the face of trying obstacles.

Afterward there was the onrush of hearty handshaking and booming congratulations, with happy cast members pretending nonchalance as they enjoyed warmhearted pats on the back. It was not condescending. A social case worker in the audience commented, "You wouldn't believe it if you didn't see it with your own eyes." A volunteer declared loudly, "I came out of duty, prepared to be bored, but I really enjoyed it! I was so moved—it was like a professional performance." A cottage mother, wiping tears from her eyes, said, "I had the feeling they were acting out their own yearnings—it was so real."

The next day the director's telephone rang incessantly,

bearing congratulatory messages. More than one caller caught himself indulging in a professional critique of the interpretations of the characters, and suddenly reminded himself that these were not professional actors but merely adolescents, and disturbed adolescents at that.

A happy throng of cast members, stage crew, helpers, ushers, and costumers reveled at the cast party following the performance. Enemies became friends, antagonisms were buried, everybody loved everybody. A spirit of happy contentment reigned over the campus that night.

From a professional and artistic point of view, a letter arrived from a noted local actor, who wrote he was "amazed at how well such a young group handled so challenging a play . . . they did not break character once. . . ."

Upon request, the play was given a "command" performance the following summer for the board of directors of the institution, with essentially the same emotional effect.

How was all this accomplished? How was it possible to obtain an organized, disciplined effort on the part of the eleven actors plus the four members of the stage crew? How were they motivated to devote most of the summer evenings for five weeks prior to performance in rehearsals and a great deal more time in studying lines and engaging in other related activities in connection with this project?

To gain some understanding of the task involved it would be important to take a cursory glance at the residential treatment center setting.

The Residential Treatment Center Setting

It is not our intention to undertake a full-length description of residential treatment here. We feel, however, that some information about the type of children, the aims and objectives, and a general idea of the over-all program is essential if one is to understand how play production as a project fits into a therapeutic milieu, as a residential treatment center is often designated.

This is a setting in which the problems of emotionally disturbed children, some of them designated as delinquent, are treated. The nation-wide concern for both has been publicized enough to warrant some examination here. These are children who, by and large, feel they are not wanted and not worth while. They are children with low self-esteem, who are bewildered and confused, who are what Fritz Redl and David Wineman so simply and aptly termed *Children Who Hate*.[1] These children often express their bewilderment and anger through behavior which becomes a problem to the adults who are responsible for these unhappy youngsters—their parents, teachers and sometimes judges and probation officers.

We shall describe such children and some of their behavior shortly in our discussion of the selection of the cast.

Of interest, too, is the fact that no longer is this problem limited to children who come from broken homes and from economically deprived families. The concern is also reaching into the middle and upper classes. In the particular treatment center described here over half the population comes from intact homes of middle-class families. As we all know, not all delinquent or emotionally disturbed children are in children's institutions. The problems of the children to be described here are but an exaggeration of the problems shown by many children. Recreational workers, public school teachers, Sunday School teachers, and others seeing children on an educational or recreational basis would certainly agree.

Because stigma still dogs the footsteps of child placement, the behavior and difficulties of a child must first have exhausted the fullest measure of parental patience and fortitude before the idea of placement can be accepted. Defiance of adults, stealing, physical aggressiveness, destruction of property, the more subtle provocation of dissension, and many other symptoms are still difficult to live with and handle, albeit in a more "objective" and "accepting" environment than the parents or community can provide.

One can easily imagine the extreme difficulties such children would present to a staff attempting any kind of organized, disciplined program activity, let alone play production, but there does exist the advantage of having such children in a twenty-four-hour living situation. It enables a group leader to be flexible and to utilize many spontaneous opportunities that occur in order to prepare children and build up enthusiasm for a project. In preparing for the production of "Golden Boy," for example, the director, who lived on the grounds of the institution, used many evenings and odd times such as Sunday mornings and early afternoon lulls in order to work with individuals and small groups. In a more formal setting, such as public school or community center, this could not have been so flexibly or so frequently arranged.

The definition of treatment varies as much as the settings, the staffs, the policies, and the populations vary over the country, in which treatment centers exist and are developing. We believe with Fritz Redl that a modern treatment center is more than "a children's home with good treatment services built in. . . ." [2] It is, rather, a "residential setting with a total treatment design" [3] in which "every phase of it must not only be 'supportive' of the basic treatment we take on but must become an integral part of it . . . the question of which arts and crafts material are being picked and how the workshop is being handled can be as much actual 'treatment' as . . . 'what the psychiatrist may have said in an interview.' " [4]

The concept of treatment held at this particular institution is one involving the total child. If one accepts this concept of totality, the everyday program and activities suddenly loom in importance and significance.

Since treatment takes place in an around-the-clock setting, we would divide the time for the program in which we attempt to achieve total treatment into, roughly, four categories:

1. *Time for activities which are "antiseptic."* [5] Here would be included time for activities such as movies, television, and other programming in which the main object consists of insuring that nothing takes place which might impede the progress or the process of treatment. Though we subscribe to the idea of totality, we realistically must take the pragmatic view here that on a seven-day, twenty-four-hour daily living basis, such times cannot possibly be avoided.

2. *Time for activities which develop values and standards or correct those deemed harmful.* These would consist of routines and such responsibilities as chores and work, through which a child is imbued with a feeling for such traits as order, cleanliness, punctuality.

3. *Time for activities which educate and enrich.* These would be provided by the school and the recreation and club activities in which skills are learned and knowledge gained through participation in them.

4. *Time for activities which are therapeutic.* These would include discussions with social case workers and/or psychiatrists regarding the children's own difficulties, and any other activity which makes them look at themselves more realistically. The ultimate goal is in gearing the total treatment in such a way that the child will be helped to face his own problems and his own part in creating or intensifying them, understand the environmental pressures and realities which have brought him pain and distress, and gain the inner strength to withstand these pressures. It is this therapy which constitutes the ultimate treatment of a treatment center and distinguishes this setting from the general children's homes for dependent and neglected children. In the final analysis, it is this goal which must be achieved if the help a child in trouble receives is to be basic and lasting.

But to get to this point—"Ah! That is the rub!" One can seldom approach it directly. It requires wide excursions, by-passing, and just plain patient waiting. The clinician, there-fore, is concerned not only with his specialized treatment area but also with all the roads that may lead to it—the total program in the institution.

To the degree, then, that programming can bridge these four categories, to that degree do we achieve total treatment. To the extent that mere time-filling activity can be replaced by more meaningful activity, can be made more enriching, associated with standards, or related to the child's own awareness of his personal problems and goals, to that extent does the environment become a therapeutic milieu where the total living is resident treatment. Thus one can see why a treatment institution is ever on the alert to find new forms of activity which may develop into therapeutic media, in the sense that they blaze trails to the clinic.

With this background in mind, we will go on to describe how the production of "Golden Boy" fits into this concept of total treatment. We should remind the reader, however, that the main focus of this study is still on the general use-fulness of play production, rather than being an attempt to prove that this first undertaking was a specifically designed therapeutic plan. It was gratifying to note that indications for such usefulness did emerge. The illustration of a treat-ment center is used primarily because the intimate knowledge of each individual which was available before, during, and after the play, constitutes, in a sense, a laboratory in which the effects on these individuals could be carefully observed and evaluated. Consequently, it is hoped that conclusions might be drawn from this experience which might be of value not only in the more systematic and intensive use of this medium as part of treatment but primarily in its wider ap-plication to more general settings, since the fundamental approach to play directing could be the same.

Getting the Drama Group Started

It is all very well to talk about the values of play production, but how does one get a play started? How can one instil into a group of youngsters the motivation to put forth the effort required by such a project? And after one succeeds in getting it started, how can the interest be maintained over the necessarily long haul? It is with justification that our staff had misgivings as to the ultimate achievement of a successful play production with our youngsters, for the obstacles to successful performance were the very problems of hyperactivity, daydreaming, and short attention span which had something to do with their being sent to the institution in the first place. Among the many manifestations of disturbance, for example, was the inability to postpone gratifications. And play production, with its many rehearsals, many of them by necessity long and laborious, requires a maximum of such postponement.

One of the principles upon which a treatment center operates is that nothing succeeds like success. The business of resident treatment, in a way, is that of providing successes, of building up the individual's self-esteem, of helping him to gain the inner strength to face problems. The writer started with the idea, therefore, that before one can set his sights on a big success, he needs to provide first a "smell of success." Because social group work and modern education favor the principle that program cannot be effectively imposed on a group of individuals, one must become, in a sense, a catalytic agent, establishing the conditions for programming in such a way that the group itself will not only want the program but will feel that the members are initiating it. This is especially true of older adolescents, who need only a suggestion from an adult to provoke them into rejecting and even belittling it.

The writer started, therefore, by planting seeds, mentioning in casual conversation to a few boys on several occasions that if they ever wanted to do anything like putting on a play, he would be glad to work with them on it, as he used to be a play director once upon a time. It was not too long before an opportunity presented itself. One of the boys, Eddie, had written a mystery play, a take-off on "Dragnet." In showing it to a few boys, they conceived the idea of presenting it to the campus. One of the boys remembered the writer's offer and approached him for help in direction.

The play was only a ten-minute skit requiring four rehearsals, and it was presented as part of a monthly campus-wide program. It gave the boys a taste of the creative approach, however, and the cast members as well as the audience were impressed with the unusual polish and finesse of the performance. The cast enjoyed its success thoroughly. Moreover, the cast party held at the director's apartment added a glowing aftermath to the performance. Doing pantomimes and playing imitations games, drinking soda pop, and cracking nuts—all added up to a most enjoyable total experience.

The boys wanted more. Now they suggested something big—a full play or a musical. A Dramatic Club was organized at which the writer was "elected" their director. It was decided to read a few plays and then vote on which should be produced. The director agreed that the club should have a choice in the selection of the play but reserved the right of veto if he did not like it personally, reasoning that a good job of directing could be done only if the director liked the play.

However, when "Golden Boy" was read, it was an instantaneous, unanimous choice. How wonderful it is to be in a position where one is pressured into doing something he had been wanting to do all the time! Among those taking part in "Golden Boy" were Joe, Tokio, Siggie, Mr. Bonaparte, Roxy, and Eddie—all of whom had taken part in the

"Dragnet" skit. Others like Moody and Lorna, who had resisted taking part in the skit, were convinced by its success that they too wanted a try at this activity. In this manner was gathered the cast for our first presentation.

The following summer the revival of the play came about through a cottage group meeting, a self-government type of weekly meeting, held by our oldest adolescent boys' cottage.

The topic of discussion was ways and means to raise money for repairing the pool table and for the cottage to go on an overnight pleasure trip. Various ideas such as an auction, card party, and raffle were suggested. Joe took the floor and scoffed, "Card parties! That's just another excuse for getting donations. We ought to do something where someone *gets* something for their money." Thus was the repeat performance production of "Golden Boy" born. (In the meantime, the director had already been made aware of the board's request for the repeat presentation. Combining the two requests presented no difficulty.) Of course, the success of the first performance further attracted other candidates. There were many more children who tried out for parts the second time than there were parts available.

Starting Drama in a Community Center

Getting a drama group started in a community center can also be accomplished with a small taste of success as a beginning. The writer, for example, was a member of a drama group where it was the usual pattern to start the season's activities by first meeting with a small nucleus of the group to plan a grand opening-of-the-season affair. This affair would consist of a program featuring a one-act play or a few skits, a talk or a demonstration by a modern dance instructor, a fencer, or a playwright. The affair was utilized to explain the group's activities and to announce try-outs for a forthcoming production. The success of the skits and the one-acts stimulated interest in others and thus kept up the membership and support of the group.

FOOTNOTES

1. Fritz Redl and David Wineman, *Children Who Hate* (Glencoe, Ill.: The Free Press, 1951).

2. Fritz Redl and David Wineman, *Controls from Within* (Glencoe, Ill.: The Free Press, 1952), p. 41.

3. *Ibid.*

4. *Ibid.*

5. This is Fritz Redl's word by which he means that if any activity cannot be helpful, it should at least not be harmful.

CHAPTER SIX

Techniques and Methods of Direction

IN THE CHAPTERS on "A Christmas Carol" we attempted to describe the step-by-step process of directing a play creatively. In this chapter it is our aim to highlight some of the techniques and methods of direction. The process and method of working with disturbed adolescents is essentially no different from that used in working with the so-called normal young adult. The differences that do exist are only in degree. One needs a much greater degree of sensitivity when he is dealing with disturbed children than he does in working with college students. One must be especially alert and attuned to moods and tensions. One must know the individuals.

The step-by-step process used in directing "Golden Boy" followed closely the steps in "A Christmas Carol," starting with the understanding of the play, delving into the meanings of the lines, studying the characters, associating lines with movements, working for a run-through, followed by the director's role as trial audience with critiques, through dress rehearsal, to performance.

At one of the first rehearsals it was found helpful to the understanding of the play to tell the story in round-robin style. This was an aid in helping to clear up the sequence of events and to fix the specific entrances of the various characters.

Relieving Tension

Another rehearsal was designed especially as a tension reliever. This was a rehearsal held in the apartment of the director as a television viewing party, in which the cast and the director watched a play on the Goodyear Playhouse program on a Sunday evening. The director used this opportunity to call attention to techniques used, such as significant pauses, turning on lines. He called attention to group interplay, pointing out instances in which actors were absorbed and listened to others.

After the television performance, around cokes and sandwiches, a general discussion was led by the director. Many actual similarities in lines between the play just seen and "Golden Boy" were noted. The idea that one should be himself was one of the main themes of the television play, and it was compared to Joe's lines in which he says, "You have to be what you are," and "I was a real sparrow but I wanted to be a fake eagle." These lines became much more meaningful to the group after the discussion.

The television play concerned a father-daughter relationship in which the father was so overprotective of the daughter that he had effectively prevented her from marrying. The plot dealt with the romance between this daughter, already over thirty years of age, and a man who was also a lonesome soul.

In discussing the overprotectiveness of the father, Anna, Joe's sister, immediately blurted out, "That was the trouble with my own father too. He wouldn't let anyone come close to me except himself." The director did not pursue this topic in the group discussion, merely commenting that it is an in-

teresting fact that problems are not unique. But this reaction
was reported to the girl's case worker, as were many others.

Here is a good example where a director could have been
led into the area of group therapy if he were not careful or
if he had a need to be overly curious. For he could quite
naturally have followed such a spontaneous outburst of the
girl with further questions about her relationship to her father. This, however, would have been a violation of his
assigned task, which was here the production of an artistic
success of a play. Only questions and discussion having
pertinence to the achievement of success are valid. Any
further probing into the girl's personal life would have been
irresponsible.

The director went on to ask which problem the group
considered more significant—Joe's problem or that of the
daughter in the television program. A lively, stimulating discussion ensued, in which both problems were evaluated.
Most of the cast members thought Joe's problem was more
important because it was more universal, being that of the
conflict between material and cultural values, but the girls
in the group seemed to be more affected by the problem
presented in the father-daughter relationship.

Preparation and Anticipation

All of us find it hard to adjust to surprises. Children instinc-
tively know the art of preparing their parents beforehand.
"You are going to be real mad at me," they begin, and by the
time they conclude their story, the facts are often much less
serious than the parent had been led to expect, and the result is likely to be a milder form of punishment than might
have been called forth otherwise. Neurotic and upset individuals can even be panicked by the unexpected. Social work
teaching, for example, stresses the value of preparation, es-

pecially for an experience that is bound to have unpleasant aspects.

The director here too observed this principle in anticipating beforehand and spelling out as specifically as possible the difficulties and frustrations the cast was likely to encounter. Coupled with this approach was the director's confidence in himself and assurance to the cast that they could rise to the occasion, that he had faith in them. This procedure was followed not only in relation to the total project, but also in each rehearsal. The following example describes the director's opening remarks to the cast at the time of the first rehearsal:

"Kids, I want you to know what you are in for. You asked me to direct this play for you, and I'm glad to do it. But I hate to do anything like this unless it's done right. I mean like real professionals. There is no better feeling in the world than after putting something like this together. By the same token, though, there is nothing stinkier and more sour if it's done poorly. But success won't fall into your laps like manna from the skies. You have to work for it and work hard. You may think I'm a fairly nice guy now. But I guarantee you there will be times you'll get so irritated with me you'll hate me, because after we get into it I'm going to be a slavedriver. Oh, we'll end up pals again, but I believe you want a good play, not just some cute little thing we do at a party. After all, you are asking hundreds of people to spend money and their good time to share an experience with you. You've got to give them an experience. I'm sure—at least some of you have complained to me often enough—that you don't want anyone to come out just to do you a favor. All right! If you want to do this like professionals, you are going to have to give up things. I'll try to work it at first that you don't miss your ball playing or your movies. But there will come a time when the play is going to have to come first and everything else will go by the board, including some sleep.

"Now, I think we can have a play such as this place has

never seen before. I've got complete confidence in each one of you and I know what I'm talking about. I've had a great deal of experience directing plays before and, well—I'm a darn good director. At least I haven't had a real flop yet. It's just a fact. You know I don't brag.

"And I promise you this. You'll always know the truth from me because I don't believe in kidding someone that he's good when he really isn't. Actually, I think you can do better than amateur adults because you're not so set in your ways. You're more flexible and imaginative. [This was true, to the director's astonishment.] But whether you can go through the grind like an adult, that you have to decide. Today is our first rehearsal. It will take twenty-four more in the next five weeks. I'm warning you again, there will be times when you will ask yourself how you ever let yourself in for something like this. We don't have to do this, you know. Before we even get started, if there is anyone who thinks this will be too much for him, now is the time to drop out. I wouldn't blame you. Believe me, it's going to be really rough and maybe you'd rather not get involved."

Some questions are asked by cast members about when rehearsals will be held as well as about other points of procedure. But no one takes the hint. Now the director quickly moves in with some reassuring remarks, anticipating that what really worries most of the cast is learning lines, although no one has mentioned it.

"O.K. A few more things. Learning lines is the least of my worries. I don't want you to even start learning lines. That will come later in the game after you thoroughly understand the meanings and the whole play. Before we get through, you will know exactly what line you stand on and what line you walk on; that will make them easier to learn. But it's what goes on between the lines that constitutes the real acting.

"Another thing, kids. I know that everyone wants to be a director. Now I don't mind different ideas, but there can be only one director and, for better or worse, this time that's me. Agreed?

"One more thing before we start reading the play. This is going to be extra time for me as well as for you. I just can't waste time being a disciplinarian. It's going to be hard to sit quiet, I know, especially later on when I block and some of you will have long spaces of time when you will have nothing to do. But you're just going to have to do it. No horsing around. It's gotta be that way, and you're going to have to handle that part of it yourselves. We don't want kid stuff in our drama group. Otherwise, we might as well not even start. O.K.?"

Radiating Confidence

It will be noted that the director made a special point of the confidence he had in himself. This was based on his conviction that even more important than a warm relationship between the director and the cast members is the supreme confidence the director radiates to them, which was reflected in their own confidence and security. Also providing security was the statement that there would be twenty-five rehearsals. Although this number was somewhat arbitrary, it did give the cast a concrete goal for which to strive. Security giving too was the knowledge that they would eventually know exactly on what lines they would stand and walk.

It was customary for each session to begin with the director's run-down of what would be taking place. A few examples follow:

"Today we will take Scenes 4 and 5. It's going to be kind of tiresome because we have to experiment a lot with different positions and movements. You will wonder why I can't make up my mind."

"Anna, you might as well settle down to some long waiting periods. It's going to be boring. If you want to get some fresh air, do it, but be sure you're here for your scene."

Another regular pattern of this process of direction was some anticipating statement as follows:

"Kids, I'm going to be real pesty now and keep interrupting this scene. I know how exasperating this can be but don't worry. It's all part of the game. You're doing all right."

It was interesting to note how often cast members would rush over at the conclusion of a scene to ask anxiously whether they had done well. A by-word of the director came known to be, "It's going according to schedule."

There was some proof that this technique of anticipating and preparing beforehand worked as cast members themselves frequently pointed out that they had been amply prepared. Often a boy would grin, "You warned us!"

Giving Criticism

One of the most ticklish tasks in working with insecure, troubled children is that of giving criticism. The chief role of the director is precisely that of discovering weaknesses as well as strengths and pointing these up, if one is to achieve success. How to give criticism without increasing insecurity and causing discouragement requires the utmost sensitivity and skill. Actually, one of the most potent tools in working with the adolescent is the challenge. But it must be hurled with no trace of sneer or ridicule. It must contain within it the firm belief and faith in the actor's ability to measure up to expectations. Part of such a technique consists of using evidences from their own performances in other rehearsals or at least in their living experiences to support the conviction that they can also do it in the scene being criticized.

"Roxy, I don't get a reaction from you when Mr. Bonaparte announces that Joe plays the violin. He might as well have said that he plays the juke box for all it seemed to mean to you."

Roxy interrupts, arguing that he did react the right way. The director shrugs and comments:

"I can't change the hard facts of life. I'm the audience. You can't get mad at me because I failed to see your reaction. It's your job to convince me without a doubt that what is going through your mind at that moment is 'Darn it, there go my dreams again!' " Now, much more earnestly, "I know you can do it. Look at the way you react to Lorna when she tries to put in her two cents about Joe. That's what I call a lifelike scene. If anyone would walk into the room not knowing this is a rehearsal, they would have really believed you don't think much of women around an office, much less about their opinion of fighters. Can't you get absorbed that way here too? O.K. Let's try it again."

Challenge

Adolescents will always oblige with more noise and more spirit when asked, unless they are out to challenge the adult deliberately.

"Kids, everything you did was right except for one thing." The director pauses, then shouts, "Spirit! Enthusiasm! Energy! Sincerity! Conviction! Come on, kids! This is as flat as a pancake. We've got to hear you. We've got to believe you. Give out! If we told you there would be an extra chapel service this week, you'd know how to raise your voices. Get into it! Let's hear these rafters shake!"

Sensitivity to Frustration Tolerance

Along with challenge and support goes a sensitivity to frustration tolerance. There were rehearsals which were abruptly adjourned when it was noticed that tensions were mounting above the danger point. There were situations also which demanded triggerlike reassurance and poise on the part of the director. During one especially wearing repetition of a scene Joe's temper finally exploded when Tokio made a late entrance for his scene. He was already chasing Tokio, raging with frustration, when the director grabbed Joe and held on. Ruffling his hair and patting him on the back, he calmly assured him, "You're doing all right. No need to worry. You're coming along fine. I tell you, right on schedule." Then, as Joe was still muttering vehement intentions, he went on, "See, I told you you could get mad. Now . . ." assuming a serious, studied air, "if you can hold on to this anger and throw it into that scene where Moody ridicules your name and your eyes . . ." This brought a chorus of laughter from all over the auditorium. Joe grinned sheepishly, and the tension was relieved.

The Trauma of the First Run-Through

Just as in "A Christmas Carol," the first run-through of the whole play was here too a crucial time. For the strongest of us, the sudden realization that lines so neatly learned in our living rooms do not float out readily on the stage when they need to, brings a panicky feeling. One can imagine how let down and terribly discouraged disturbed adolescents could feel at such a realization. Such an experience could become even traumatic. Even though the cast was prepared in advance in the manner described above, it could only cushion the shock of missed lines, botched-up scenes, panicky blacking out, and numerous breaking of scenes and character. The description of what transpired at the conclusion of this rehearsal reads as follows:

> The cast is seated forlornly on the stage. One could well imagine that their unspoken thoughts were probably, "We were fools to think we could do it." The director, taking his time, is dictating final notes to his helper. Now he looks over the cast quizzically. The next few moments are crucial. They will not guarantee to make the play but they can certainly break it. Since he had been rather harsh in insisting the play keep going, lines or no lines, and had been impatient with poor back-stage discipline, the cast was set for some rather

caustic remarks by the director. Instead, he calmly announces, "Kids, you've got a show."

They look up in surprise, ears perked. The director goes on, "I'm not worried. I know that a million things happened that shouldn't have happened, and there were things I would never recognize as part of the play. But that's nothing. We'll fix all that up. I'm not worried. But there were some touching moments too when I was really moved. Actually, you don't even realize when you're good! Joe, I could have shot you. Here you build up this beautiful climax where you reach the greatest height of expression so far—so just because you forgot one line, you throw up the whole works. What if you missed a line? Do you think the audience would ever know it? The audience hasn't studied the lines. They hear you for the first time, and unless you advertise to them that you forgot a line, they would never know it, but they would have been moved to tears if you had just gone on, stayed in the play. You have only one job to do, to express the thoughts of Joe Bonaparte and thereby stir the audience's emotions. You actually did it. Do you realize it? . . .

"I told you before the rehearsal that all these mistakes were going to be made. I've seen adults with much more experience do even worse with their first run-through. But that's why I hope you can see now why it is vital to have at least four complete run-throughs before dress rehearsal. That's what it takes to get you all comfortable in your character so that you can throw the lines out without even worrying about it, and so that they come really natural."

In order to have these needed run-throughs, plus special rehearsals on weak scenes, the cast agrees to reserve Labor Day for the play, which means giving up visits, a planned boat ride and movies.

One of the cast members told his case worker later that the phrase, "You've got a show!" was the turning point for the whole cast. They had a resurgence of confidence and determination and came back with renewed vigor for the rest of the rehearsals, now devoted primarily to run-throughs with written criticism afterward by the director.

Perhaps it need not be mentioned that in none of the final performances was the audience ever aware of any lines missed or of any break in the play. This was in itself an achievement and a tribute to the group spirit and co-operation.

The Role of the Director at Performance

The role of the director just before and during the performances differed in this setting from that of the college where "A Christmas Carol" was produced. In the latter setting, he began to retire from the scene, confining his activity to relaxing the actors, speaking to the cast briefly, merely assuring them that this was just another rehearsal, and watching the performance from the audience.

The cast of "Golden Boy," however, needed much more support and the security the director's presence insured. His speech to the cast was used as a final step in building group spirit and in stirring them to the emotional depths of which they were capable and on which, in the final analysis, the success of the play depended. His speech reads as follows:

"Kids, gather around me here. Get comfortable. I want a final few words with you. My job is done. I'll be back here with the book, but I won't need it. In a few moments you will be appearing before your first full audience. Then your job will be done. The fact that there is an audience needn't make a particle of difference to you. Remember the fourth wall: the audience doesn't exist. You know that. You know that you've got a show. You've had one ever since the second runthrough. I have said that the performance is rarely better than the best rehearsal. On the other hand, once you have a show, you don't lose it either. One performance may be better than another, but the basic accomplishment is still there, just the same as if you had built something tangible. It's been a long grind, kids, and you've learned a lot. It's in your muscles now, and you won't unlearn it now just because it's a performance in front of an audience. There is one thing that's more important, though, than all the training and learning you have absorbed, and that's what you've got down here (points to heart), the feeling that you pour out of your heart. If you have ever been lonesome in your life, be lonesome now. If you ever felt snarly and irascible and irritated, feel snarly and irascible and irritated now. If you ever had a deep longing or yearning, yearn now. If there was ever a tear in your eyes for someone else's suffering and anguish (there was now one in the director's), let it be there now. Get in the mood now. Work together, listen to each other, hang on to each other's every thought, absorb yourself into the play and into the troubles of the Bonapartes and the Lornas and the Moodys. And you'll be great. I'm already proud of each one of you. Go at this like another rehearsal, and make this the best one yet. I know you're going to have a rare, thrilling experience which we will all remember the rest of our lives. Good luck!"

After the handshaking and big bear hugs, all become sober and quiet. Is there ever a moment in life comparable in richness to the anticipatory tension back-stage before the curtain rises! And is there a sigh that breathes more relief than at the pulling of the curtain and the delivery of the opening lines of the play?

CHAPTER SEVEN

Significance to the Participants

LIKE THE DIRECTOR, those in the audience who knew something about the individual participants in "Golden Boy" were especially moved and, as it were, basked in a certain reflected glory. Unlike the example of "A Christmas Carol," where the director had no knowledge of the individuals prior to the first rehearsal, it was vitally necessary here, with disturbed, mistrustful children, for the director to have a good understanding of each individual and a relationship already established before undertaking such a project.

Time and space do not permit a full description of all the individuals, but the following description of three of the cast members' experiences in this play and the meaningfulness to them may give an idea of the rare thrill that must have been experienced by those who had struggled with all the youngsters through temper tantrums and tears, destruction and defiance, car stealings and run-aways. In less detail other individuals will be described in the chapter, "The Player and the Part" and throughout other parts of this study. The individuals will be identified, as were those in "A Christmas Carol" in Chapter 3, by the names of the characters they portrayed.

Moody, the Fight Manager

Moody was a rather wiry, dark-complexioned, black-haired boy, who had been at the institution for about four years, although during this time he had, on one occasion, been tried in a foster home where his demanding attitude and his fidgety restlessness could not be tolerated, and from which he was, therefore, returned to the institution. He was sixteen years old and the only full orphan residing at the treatment center, his adoptive parents having been killed in an accident when he was eight years old. Although electroencephalograms did not yield positive evidence, there was suspicion of brain damage deduced from his behavior and from psychological testing. At any rate, he had been dealt with as such. His over-all IQ was 85 and he functioned on a dull, normal level. He had suffered temper tantrums and outbursts of rage which were so severe that he frothed at the mouth. He was so completely out of control that it required three adults, on one occasion, to contain him.

He was unable to stick to a task for more than a few minutes at a time. He was slothful in his personal habits and hygiene. Cottage parents wore themselves out nagging him to take his showers and to finish his household chores. He dawdled and slouched around the grounds. He was a boy who suffered failure after failure; in his four years at the institution he could not point to one successful achievement. Yet he was selected not only for the play but for the prominent part of Moody and had even been considered for the largest part of Joe.

One of the director's first disciplinary tasks shortly after joining the staff of this institution had been to return the boy from a neighborhood drugstore where he was discovered attempting to steal a few bottles of wine. Through the ensuing rather fervent argument that took place in ordering him restricted to the cottage, the director was struck with the boy's way of dramatizing his situation. He stalked up and down the living room, pacing agitatedly, sinking into the couch to bewail his fortune and his fate, then suddenly springing up again to renew heatedly his charges against the institution. He's so sick and tired of this place! Nobody understands him—nobody! He allowed himself a long pause. Then, subsiding, he wryly conceded that he really doesn't blame anyone but himself; he really is wrong and, well, it's all right; he guesses if he has to take it, he'll take it. He stared out of the window, presenting a picture of thoroughly cleansed repentance—with one ear cocked hopefully awaiting the softening of the punishment which should logically follow such heartwarming remorse, especially by an "understanding" adult. Though the director did not oblige by rising to the occasion, he was moved and thought to himself, "If I could only get him to express himself this way on the stage, it might be the handle with which he could be helped to achieve success and gain a feeling of self-worth."

Other hints that he possessed talent for acting were in the way that he pointed up words and in his unique manner of leaning on certain expressions. He did not occupy the top rung on the ladder of popularity in the group, but he was fairly well liked by his peers because of his homely philosophical type of conversational skill. He had a facility for creating suspense and building up to climaxes.

We banked heavily, too, on the fact that he was "going steady" with Lorna, the girl who played the feminine lead, for such a circumstance heightened his motivation to put forth effort and sustain attention, and it also provided a challenge for him. With the exception of illnesses which kept him from attending some rehearsals, he maintained his interest and enthusiasm for the play throughout. Because he was so fidgety and easily distracted, he was often a disciplinary problem during rehearsals but not to the extent anticipated.

The trauma of the first run-through, described earlier, was too much for him, however. He was so frustrated at missing some lines that he almost had a temper tantrum but managed to control himself, at least to the extent of running outside to let off steam. After calming himself, he returned and objectively studied the script to determine where he had slipped.

His portrayal was the most colorful and imaginative achievement in the group. In many places he ad-libbed like a veteran and kept the play going. He fell into the spirit and was so imbued with the idea of the play as a whole that he enjoyed ad-libbing and took the liberty (a little too often for comfort) of adding a thought or two of his own. But he had no real difficulty with lines and thoroughly understood their meanings and the total play. The one exception was a scene which called for resignation but which he insisted on interpreting as defiance. He could not seem to humble himself even in a play.

Needless to say, he received a great deal of praise for his performance and was looked upon with a new respect. His feeling of accomplishment could be literally observed in his bearing. His shoulders straightened; he carried himself more erect, and his whole demeanor took on a new look of confidence. He wanted to do more acting and was disappointed that the play was presented only once during his stay at the institution. He was one of the chief campaigners for a repeat performance.

This first success led him into other activities. He became the editor of the campus newspaper and developed an interest in painting. It was he who provided the imagination whenever decorating was needed in his cottage.

He also developed a greater self-control. Although he subsequently became involved in a few incidents where he overturned chairs and destroyed property, these never attained the degree of violence and uncontrollable rage which had characterized his temper tantrums heretofore.

In a psychological retesting shortly after his performance in the play it was discovered that his IQ was 101.

A month before the repeat performance of the play the following summer Moody was discharged, in order to enlist in the Navy. While this account was being written he had successfully completed his boot training and had, in fact, been given an instructorship in drill.

Joe Bonaparte I, the Fighter

The Joe of the first performance was heavy-set with a flabby stomach, a lazy boy who slept late, was sloppy and dirty. In order to cast him it was necessary to change the character's weight from 133 to 193 pounds in the dialogue of the play. To many it looked incredible to assign to him the role of a fighter, for if he did not look the part physically, he was even less similar psychologically and socially. His interests were primarily intellectual and cultural. He knew the statistics about sports and filled the cottage atmosphere with boister-ous arguments about the facts of athletic achievements, but rarely did he participate in active sports himself.

He was a sixteen-year-old boy who had been in the in-stitution for two years because of serious difficulties at home, especially with his mother who openly rejected him, regard-ing him from birth as a curse and punishment from God, while she treated his older sister as a blessing. Although his father did not share such an attitude, he was placid, weak, inept, and unable to counteract the mother's emasculation of the boy.

Joe reacted with all kinds of attention-getting devices. When acquiring the status of a model student at school did not bring him the mother's approval, he rather suddenly at the age of fourteen turned to little delinquencies, especially stealing from the mother's purse.

In the semester prior to the presentation of the play he had failed in school and had withdrawn from all activities in an almost premeditated design of punishing himself. It was pathetic to see him devour such books as *War and Peace* but refuse obstinately to do his required reading for school.

The assignment to the role of Joe, then, was made despite the dissimilarities of characteristics. Some of the reasons for such casting will be discussed under that heading later. It is enough to say for the moment that his immediate grasp of the character in the reading try-outs, which instantly moved the director and the rest of the cast, and his own great desire for the part were major considerations in this decision.

Joe was one of the hardest working members of the cast, ready at any time of day or night to rehearse. He stimulated many line rehearsals and spontaneous discussions in the cottage. He did falter a few times and there were some periods of silliness bordering on giddiness. There were also some instances in which he told the director that he didn't think he could go through with the play, but basically these were appeals for reassurance, which he received.

Our expectations of him were more than fulfilled. He provided the feeling tone around which the other cast members mobilized and which profoundly moved the audience. In a way, he occupied the role of the unsung hero who plays on the line of a winning football team, but who does not share the spotlight with the halfback whose dazzling runs would not be possible without the burly guard or tackle to open up a hole or throw a crucial block. He was like the flashing comedian's straight man who is every bit as important on the team, for without the foil and the tone which he provides, the comedian's comedy would be lost.

Though Joe was not among those singled out as one of the best stars, the director knew, the cast knew, and most of all

Joe realized that he carried the bulk of the emotional tone of the play. As a result, he grew in stature and respect, particularly among his own cottage peers. His participation in the play seemed to mellow him and give him a new lease on life. He took much more leadership in the cottage and initiated many activities. His return to school was marked by a new determination and a resurgence of good grades. At the end of the semester following the play, strengthened by a new sense of worthwhileness, he returned home to live with his family, confident that he could stand up under his mother's unchanged attitude of ridicule. It was sad to note, in passing, that the mother not only did not come to see the play but had managed, through intrigue, to keep other relatives from attending. The stigma of the institution was unacceptable to her. The father, however, had been a visitor at a rehearsal and had expressed a great deal of pride in his son.

Perhaps the best evidence of what meaning the play had for this boy was in the fact that he wanted very much to do more acting and told the director that he felt he had gained a great deal of poise and confidence through this activity.

Worth mentioning too was the particularly good relationship he developed with the director in the process of working on the play. The special radiance with which Joe greeted the director was one of the intangible rewards for which one becomes a social worker and a director of plays. Even now Joe comes to visit and to chat. He is now in college.

Joe Bonaparte II

The casting of Joe Bonaparte for the repeat performance was in stark contrast to the first Joe. Our second Joe was perfectly suited to the part physically, since he was endowed with a fighter's body. In the scene where he comes out attired in fighter's trunks, there was an audible murmur of admiration from the audience for his beautiful physique. He was a fifteen-year-old boy, huskily built. He looked like a bull, and his hair was like a shaggy mane. Getting his hair cut was a constant bone of contention between him and his cottage mother. He was one of the most popular boys on the campus, for physical prowess is still one of the major avenues through which adolescents reach popularity and respect and also command a certain fear from their peers. He was a star player on his junior high school football and basketball teams and was proficient in all sports.

His behavior too was marked by opposite qualities of our first Joe. No petty attention-getting devices for him! He shoved, pushed, slugged, and bellowed. He was our typical "dead end kid," who is representative of a certain pattern of delinquency. He played truant from school, ran away from home, broke into homes, and stole cars. He was a boy who hit out directly against his environment, in open defiance of all authority.

When Joe was only two years old his mother had deserted, the first of a series of regular desertions. His father, a steel worker, tried to handle him by alternately placating him and then beating him. He was left to wander at will, unsupervised a great deal of the time. He shined shoes on the streets. He traveled in a gang. He came from a neighborhood in which, he told his case worker, you not only had to *act* tough; you had to *be* tough. Frantically, the father attempted a few independent placements which failed. Joe first became involved in court with a group of boys in a house-pilfering incident. Finally, after stealing a car at age thirteen, he was placed by the court in the institution.

Our intake conference was marked by hesitation in accepting this boy. Our open environment offered too many temptations to the aggressive delinquent. With no bars or gates, what would we do if he walked out? How could we enforce his acceptance of our routines? What if he said, "Make me!"

Here was a boy who, first of all, like all other adolescents, hated orders and restrictions and burned inwardly at the sight of an adult jingling change in his pocket, getting into a car of his own, and driving off without having to ask permission of anyone. Added to this typical adolescent attitude was the boy's complete lack of any strong identification ties, of a mother's affection and solicitude, of any social training. Our hesitance about our ability to help here was understandable. Moreover, we knew that such a boy would not be likely to respond to case work or psychiatric therapy.

Our main hope for treatment was in the possible group influence. If this boy had no respect for adult authority, there was the possibility that he might be influenced by his peers and that through group pressure and group activity he might be helped to learn a new way of life where he could develop his talents and ultimately be amenable to case work therapy. However, as the group looked to us at that time, the prospect of help through that quarter too was bleak. A good group needs natural leadership from within and strong friendship ties. Our analysis of the group at that time disclosed a divided leadership. One faction was led by a boy whose influence was negative, who had a disdain for adults and for the institution. Another faction was composed of a group whose main interests were cultural. We were, therefore, quite concerned that Joe would fall into the negative group. However, after considerable deliberation, because we saw strong potentials and some strong interests in the boy, we decided to take a calculated risk.

The first three months of Joe's stay could be described as a "honeymoon period," which institution workers have come to expect—the early conforming behavior that characterizes some children until they evaluate the environment, "case the joint," so to speak. Though he already disclosed a certain uncouthness and needed to be nagged about his chores and his personal hygiene, on the whole he spent this time sitting

on the steps, surveying the scene, and arriving at the conclusion that "this is a good deal"—in contrast to what he
would have had at the state training school to which he
surely would have been committed had not this institution
been made available to him. He was quite tight-lipped. The
only communication he had known all his life was the fist
and the threat. Needless to say, he did not keep his case
work appointments, and on the rare occasion when he did
appear, he was unable to talk about himself or his problems.

Black or White Thinking

Joe's behavior at this time was further characterized by
his "black or white" thinking. He had come to the institution with the idea that adults either were tough or were
suckers. There was nothing in between. He began to be
quite argumentative. He argued about his budget; he argued
about routines; he argued about limitations—and always in
terms of black or white, just or unjust. There was no bend
to him. On one occasion he was involved in a serious in-
fraction of the rules with another boy. In the handling of this
situation, it developed that the other boy received no specific
punishment while Joe was restricted to his cottage for the
week end. He was enraged. Hours were spent trying to explain the reason for this disparity. But he was bullish and
refused to carry out his restriction. That week end he left the
campus. Three times the writer personally chased him in his
car to bring him back, convinced that this was the best way
of showing in action our concern for him and our interest in
developing a relationship. The ray of light that existed here
was that he did come back upon firm insistence. There would
have been no way of forcing him back physically had he
resisted.

Another incident in which the writer had become the disciplinarian was one in which Joe went to the infirmary to
secure medical treatment for his leg. When he was asked to

wait in the lobby for a few moments, he became so frustrated he threw a chair through a window.

Nevertheless, he began to make a good deal of progress. After one semester in our intramural school for children unable to adjust to public school, he was transferred to an outside public school and proceeded to secure good grades and to establish good functioning relationships with the principal and teachers.

He began to take a greater interest in institutional life and blossomed out with many talents. It is unusual to find a boy who not only is good in sports but also has a good singing voice and enjoys singing, a boy who likes to paint and draw, loves to improvise on the piano or drum. Fortunately Joe found outlets for these interests on the campus. Added to his physical attributes, his sensitive smile and his identification with the group made him the most popular boy on the campus. He was not given to the usual subtleties and manipulations at which the more sophisticated delinquent is a master when involved in difficulties. On the other hand, his code would not allow him to betray a pal. He would hang his head and refuse to speak when cornered. And still throughout this period he would not talk to his case worker or face his own problems and fears.

This was a period characterized by a burning curiosity. He wanted to know, albeit rather boisterously and in a pseudothreatening manner, the meaning of every word that he couldn't understand. He became fascinated with all the administrative mechanics regarding allowances, mail, clothing, laundry; and many were the fervent complaints and debates that went on between him and various staff members.

There was a major setback. Apparently he was experiencing success too rapidly and could not rid himself of the guilt over succumbing to a decent way of life, guilt dictated by his feeling of worthlessness. He had not yet accepted himself. He was still a follower in the group, easily influenced, and the streets still held their lure and mysterious excitement for him. Four months prior to the casting of the play he was led by another youngster, who was subsequently committed to a state training school, into stealing a car for the ostensible purpose of heading south. They were picked up by the police when they had an accident and damaged the car. It took the combined efforts of the superintendent, case worker, and school principal to prevail upon the court to give him one more chance at the institution.

His return from the detention home was marked by a greater sobriety. Our fears of swagger and boastfulness which sometimes surround such a return did not materialize. He quickly readjusted and entered campus life with renewed vigor and enthusiasm. He became increasingly popular and was elected the president of the campus self-governing body. But he was still closemouthed and did not open up to his case worker.

It had already been noticed that Joe's curiosity had been piqued by the play when it had been presented the previous year. He had watched a few rehearsals and had made some astute comments. He had objected, for example, to Mr. Bonaparte's use of dialect (as had the director in view of Mr. Bonaparte's inability to sustain the dialect throughout the play). When it was decided to give the play a second time, he seemed eager to participate, and, upon being offered a part in the play, he was quite interested.

Joe's burning curiosity, evidenced from the very beginning of rehearsals, was assurance to the director that the role would be sustained and the approach to the characterization would be one of maturity and humility. Joe simply refused, and in this he was encouraged by the director, to carry on any dialogue unless he fully understood the meanings of what he was saying.

When we reached the phase of rehearsals in which the cast first got on its feet, the struggles really began. Given wide latitude, at first, for using movements natural to him, Joe fidgeted and paced endlessly. The director allowed this to go on for a long time, not daring to distract him from his gropings with lines and meanings and, perhaps, his own struggle to fit himself into such a venture. Only when he was comfortably esconced, when he had "taken on" some of the character and felt some security in the part did the director begin to tamper with his physical actions. He broke up the pacing, found things for him to hold and grab and on which to lean, developed a hands-on-hips major gesture. It was a slow process which went on almost into dress rehearsal time.

Another pattern of Joe's revealed itself during the latter phase of rehearsals when the stress was, as illustrated in "A Christmas Carol," on no stopping, on carrying on with one's own lines, if need be, so that the unity and totality of the play would be maintained and the illusion unbroken. Joe had a difficult time, at first, to stay in character. He became easily frustrated and gave up apologetically. The director spent a great deal of time discussing with him this tendency of "throwing in the sponge."

"So you thought this play acting business didn't take guts and stamina!" he laughingly chided him.

"You said it, man!" grinned Joe in concurrence, upon which he plunged back into the fray and went at the business of rehearsing with renewed determination.

Becoming Creative

Soon he began to develop unique touches of his own. In one of the early scenes, for example, in which Joe the character gropes for a way in which he can face his father with his decision to become a fighter and give up the violin playing which has been his father's dream for him, he can do it only by becoming overly aggressive and defiant (remarkably similar to Joe, the adolescent). He finally ends with a speech directed at his father:

"Do you know there are men who have wonderful things from life? Do you think they're better than me? Do you think I like the feeling of no possessions? Of learning about the world from Carp's encyclopedia? You don't know what it means to sit around here and watch the months go ticking by. Do you think that's a life for a boy my age? . . ."

At this point Joe added the exclamation "Huh!" and repeated it with a firmer, more insistent and demanding, louder, climactic "Huh!" It electrified the rest of the cast, the stage crew, and others who were watching the rehearsal, as it did the audience during the performance. One could have heard the proverbial pin drop during the pause following this climax.

At the end of the scene Joe dashed over to the director, wanting to know whether he had done all right. He couldn't quite believe that something he had created was important and good enough to be made a permanent part of the play.

Pre-Performance Chills

As the time for performance drew nearer, and as he began to realize the momentousness of the task he had undertaken, Joe became more apprehensive and frightened. Finally, he admitted to the director he was scared and didn't think he could go through with it. Receiving a friendly laugh, a pat on the back, and the assurance that everything was working out according to schedule, he was obviously relieved. The director freely used his own prestige, invoking his own past experiences in pointing out that all play productions consist of these struggles and gropings and fears. But he also expressed his pleasure at Joe's realization of what was involved in producing a play, for this was itself a major step toward the project's successful consummation.

In view of and precisely because of Joe's growing apprehension and the accompanying tension building up around this, because of the very vicissitudes of play production, because it was Joe's first experience in so large a production and in this type of activity, and because he hurdled the obstacles and turned in a sound performance unmarred by any break in character, it was a remarkably enriching, ego-building experience for the boy. For him to admit apprehension was in itself a piercing of the crust of the defiant delinquent. It meant a great deal to Joe to feel that he could succeed in such an accomplishment. He was somewhat bewildered, however, and couldn't quite believe that what he did as a person naturally on the stage was actually successful acting.

In truth, his creation of the role was a rather tight-lipped, grim, withholding character, much like himself. It lacked the fervor, the feeling tone, and the wistfulness of our first Joe, which from an artistic point of view succeeded better in producing an emotional effect upon the audience. An actor creates a role from the base of his own personality, but he should at the end of the process add something to it, take on some added stature and humor, and in that sense become a more expanded individual. Our first Joe succeeded in such an expansion. The second Joe did not quite get out from under himself. But his complete understanding of the role and the play, in many ways more acute and mature than our first Joe, succeeded in broadening his vision, poked holes in many of his preconceived notions about life being all tough or all soft, introduced him to profound values and standards which are still incubating and still being assimilated. The result left him more thoughtful and even somewhat more morose. Shortly after the play was over, he began to be preoccupied with illness, expressed fears that he was becoming diabetic because he was drinking water in profuse quantities, and asked to see the doctor.

In this second performance the staff was more alert to the relationship between the dramatic activity and social case work. As has been mentioned before, Joe would not open up in his contacts with his case worker. Three weeks before the play went into rehearsal, the case worker in attempting to open up with Joe the subject of his feelings toward his mother had been rebuffed with the cry, "I haven't *got* a mother, and that's that! Don't ever mention that to me again!" One week before the play, however, he finally opened the subject himself, admitting that he had thought a lot about her but felt that even if she did reform he still wanted nothing to do with her. The case work contacts up to the time of this writing are somewhat more focused on his own personality and his own reactions to situations. The "throwing in the sponge" approach hit upon by the director in the play is used now as an opening wedge by the case worker. Most important, Joe is talking about his feelings and his problems. He is achieving well in school. He is a leader both in the cottage and the entire campus.

CHAPTER EIGHT

The Player and the Part

WE HAVE JUST HIGHLIGHTED in the case of three individuals some of their experiences from early childhood through the conclusion of their participation in the play, in an attempt to show the significance for each of them of their participation in such a project. Though the same process might be followed for many others who took part in the play, we do not wish to belabor the point but will turn at this time to another aspect of play directing.

Because the selection of the cast and the assignment of the roles to the players are of primary importance in establishing the preconditions for a successful performance, we should like to devote the following section to an examination of some of the factors that influence these choices.

In most theatre groups, both professional and amateur, the selection of a cast is made by a process known as "reading try-outs." This procedure, as the name implies, consists of a meeting at which those interested in participating in the play gather to read different selections from the play. From these readings the director can get an idea of the interpretations which prospective cast members give to characters, contrasts in voices, and the general interest and enthusiasm of the applicants for the play and the group. Naturally, added to the impression thus created on the director is any other information he may have about the individual's reputation, personality, and previous acting experience. All these factors are important in influencing his final decision.

One of the debatable questions in the problem of casting, especially in a treatment institution setting, is whether a person should play the part of a character with physical and personality traits much like his own, or whether he should play a personality different from himself. We have already begun some discussion of this point in Chapter 2 on "A Creative Approach."

Inasmuch as the title role of Joe Bonaparte was filled by two boys of such different personality types in the two separate performances of the play "Golden Boy," we have here an opportunity to examine not only theoretically but also by way of examples the arguments on either side of this question.

Casting to Physical Type

All other things being equal, this writer believes that type casting, that is, the choice of an actor according to the similarity between him and the character to be portrayed, offers the greatest opportunity for a successful performance. This principle was observed in the selection of Joe II, who, engaging in his first experience before an audience, would have failed had he tried any other role but that of Joe, which was markedly similar both in physical and personality characteristics to himself. As it was, he could not quite succeed in extracting out of the role more than what he himself was, as has already been pointed out. Although one creates a role from the base of one's personality, we hope that we are not contradicting ourselves by maintaining that the final creation should be a character somewhat broader, somewhat richer, somewhat, if you will, more profound than the individual actor himself. It was this broadening that our second Joe was unable to accomplish in his portrayal of the role. Despite this, however, the portrayal was successful in terms of audience reception.

Never is there only one reason for casting a person in a certain role, type casting notwithstanding. We were also particularly interested in getting a boy like Joe into this kind of activity because of its effect on the rest of the group and the possibility that presented itself here of breaking down the aura of femininity that surrounds such an activity as drama. We were sure too that once he could succeed in such an enterprise, a whole vista of culture would be opened to him. His participation in the play enabled us to use many opportunities for ego building, to show him that his feelings, his expressions, and his own peculiar mannerisms were important and worth while. The total significance to this boy of such participation has already been discussed.

Casting to Opposite of Physical Type

In the casting of the first Joe, on the contrary, the reader may well wonder how it was that the role of a smooth, polished, crisp, pantherlike fighter was assigned to a flabby-stomached, overweight, culturally-oriented boy. On surface glance it might even appear that the writer in this instance deserted his beliefs and fell in with the recommendations of those group workers who would advocate the giving of the part of an aggressive, shouting boss to a shy, withdrawn youngster, ostensibly for the purpose of bringing out his latent aggression.[1]

This was by no means the case. The casting of Joe I was determined by factors quite different from the so-called "mental hygiene" or "therapeutic" aspects of casting. Let us examine more carefully the actual factors which led to this choice.

As has already been stressed, this writer is of the conviction that in order for an individual to benefit from participation in a play, his experience in such an endeavor must be a successful one. The success of a dramatic performance depends in large part on the ability of the actor to move the audience emotionally. Experience has shown that one predictive criterion for such a successful effect on an audience is in the ability of the actor to move the director emotionally in the reading try-outs. In the initial reading of "Golden Boy," the cast as well as the director were instantly moved at the intense cry of Joe I which came through under the bravado. This was the most important factor determining his selection, although by no means the only factor. Apparent also at the reading try-out was Joe I's immediate understanding and grasp of the character he was to portray. This prophesied a sensitive and creative handling of the role.

Another important factor determining Joe I's selection for the part was his own intense desire for the part. Unlike others whose desire is based on no more than a superficial wish to be in the limelight, Joe's wish was realistic, based rather on an interest in taking part in a play and, in addition, a special desire to portray this particular character. In connection with this latter point, we must be aware that such an intense desire to portray a particular character must reflect, in spite of all surface appearances, some underlying identification with the character in question. Thus, in spite of Joe's differences from the traits of the fighter he was to portray, his wish for the part also bespoke similarities lying dormant which, with successful direction, might be stirred to the enrichment of the total performance.

Important also was the director's confidence in Joe's ability to carry through and sustain the role successfully. This confidence was based on the director's knowledge of his performance in a previous skit as well as observation of him in such a capacity as conducting chapel services. The role of Joe was such a large one, that it was important to have someone here who could be an inspiration, a "spark plug," for the rest of the cast. Though Joe was not particularly popular with the rest of the group, he was respected, and because of his intelligence and initiative he was the natural leader of the group in the cast. Moreover, he possessed a reliability and a maturity that could provide a pivotal security for the group.

Last, but not least, was the factor of expedience. At the time of the first casting, there was no better alternative for the role. It must be admitted, had Joe II competed for the part, he probably would have been chosen in preference to Joe I. But at the time Joe II was by no means ready for such an undertaking, nor did he show any special interest.

In view of all the factors already mentioned in favor of the selection of Joe I, therefore, the matter of his not being appropriate for the part from the point of view of type casting had to be evaluated in terms of whether, in view of his dissimilarities from the character, he might still succeed in making the role a plausible one. It was here that the creative approach paid dividends, for, in spite of our description of the fighter, there was no reason within the scope of the development of the plot for him to be so rigidly portrayed. In reality, fighters vary, not only in physical characteristics but in personality traits as well. It was possible, therefore, to adapt the character in the play to resemble more closely our potential actor. One technical adaptation, easy enough to make as it in no way affected the plot, was to change the fighter from the middle-weight to the heavy-weight class. As for the cultural orientation of our actor, this was in itself not a major difficulty because the actual conflict in the play dealt with Joe's choice between fighting and violin playing. If there were lines giving Joe's feelings about fighting, there were just as many lines where he brought out the deep effect upon him of music. Here our Joe could be most plausible.

All in all, therefore, the positive factors carried the decision not by weight of number alone but because the one outstanding negative factor could, in the opinion of the director, be effectively minimized. The success of Joe I in this role bore out this prediction.

Some Bad Guesses

In retrospect, we can point to some examples of casting which may not have been the wisest choices in terms of the relationship between the personality characteristics of the actor and the character portrayed. Our first Siggie, for instance, was a tall, thin, tight-faced boy of sixteen years. He had been a truant from school and was generally sly and constricted in his expression. Although he was bright, read a great deal, and enjoyed music and participation in sports, his somber, quiet manner was his resolution of a fatalistic acceptance of his lot in life. He was cast to play the part of Joe's brother-in-law, an outgoing, quarrelsome, insensitive, boorish cab driver, who makes a pest of himself because he cannot take "no" for an answer.

It might be logically reasoned that if one who too easily accepts his lot in life is given a part in which he fights for his place in the sun, refuses to acknowledge setbacks—lo and behold!—the person himself might start taking more of a stand for his rights. How wonderful it would be if it worked so simply! The fact is that the portrayal of Siggie was rather flat and artificial. He could not break his tendency to sing-song the lines, a reflection of his inability to change his own patterns of behavior to conform to those of the outgoing cab driver.

Casting to Emotional Temperament

Still in our mood of speculative hindsight, it occurs to us that another factor in casting is a person's readiness to undertake a particular role in terms of the kind of emotion to be expressed.

Tokio was a roundfaced, roly-poly boy, fourteen years of age, with a wide, sheepish smile. He was a striking example of a child who felt unwanted and worthless. His father, a disgruntled artist, was an egocentric, grandiose man, who sat around bewailing his fortune and his fate. To help support the family, the mother was employed full time, and she did not let up in her relentless hammering away at the father on this score. As a result of this tension-ridden home, our second Tokio reacted by petty stealing, defiance, and disobedience. When he was cast for the part, he had just returned from a two-week visit at home, which had reawakened all his confusion and bewilderment about his parents and, consequently, about himself. His attempts to convince himself against his underlying fears that he respected his parents, that he was really wanted, led him into a most diffused acting-out behavior. He talked endlessly, ran around the campus heehawing and laughing giddily, calling himself "crazy." He stayed out late at night and hurled profane insults at any passer-by. Such behavior was usually followed by a plea for punishment. On one occasion, after throwing a book at a staff member, he punished himself by getting into his pajamas and crawling into bed at 7:00 P.M.

There was a quality of such desperation to his eternal restlessness that the staff was deeply affected. We could discern clearly his cry for help, for reassurance, and for clarification of his overwhelming confusion.

When Tokio asked for a part in the play, the play was already in rehearsal, with most of the roles filled. That of Tokio remained open, however—a role calling for concern for others, understanding, and tenderness. From his knowledge of the boy, the director knew he possessed these qualities, nor was there anything in his personal appearance to counterindicate his playing this part. It was, accordingly, assigned to him.

Never was a director called upon to exercise greater patience and fortitude than in working with this boy. Most of the time he engaged in spells of silliness and was unable to sustain attention. Indeed, it was not before the final rehearsal that he was able to concentrate enough to blend himself into the play. It should be mentioned that this boy's relationship to the director, even before his participation in the play, was one of special respect and warmth. It is questionable whether he could have achieved any success without this sustaining relationship. We still marvel at his performance, which was outstanding despite all the handicaps described. Certain bits of acting were picked by the audience as memorable. He received a great deal of recognition and prestige, and his irritating behavior diminished markedly following the performance. To the time of this writing he has maintained a greater calm and seems to be enjoying a much greater stability and security.

Although it might be inferred that "all's well that ends well," the edge between failure and success was razor thin. That failure can be as harmful as success can be beneficial, points up the tremendous responsibility in a casting decision. Fortunately, the clinical team shared in these decisions, but this writer would think a long time before he would again subject a child (not to mention himself) to the great strain and expenditure of energy which was the price of this success.

In retrospect, we feel an equal success might have resulted with much less strain had the boy been cast in the part of Roxy—a role calling for sarcasm, insolence, and ridicule. We know from long experience that the pus of a wound must drain before the healing process can take over. This is as applicable to the festering of hatred and bitterness as it is to physical infections. Applying this same principle here in play production with disturbed children, it would seem best to cast a person in a part where he has the best opportunity to pour out his feelings *of the moment*. It is only after feelings are released that we can gain some perspective on life's experiences, clarify them for ourselves, and become ready to move on to more healthy, broadening, and more mature patterns of behavior. In this one experience of acting, such a release was denied Tokio. Whatever benefits he gained came from the recognition, feeling of achievement through effort, and other sources, but not from the release of feeling which overwhelmed him and interfered with his functioning generally and throughout the rehearsals.

This speculation was somewhat borne out in a recent Hanukkah program in which he portrayed the role of Antiochus, the Hitler-type Syrian king. He was eager to play this villain and seemed to gain a great deal of emotional release and a feeling of personal relief from this experience. He was a big hit in the part.

Talent

The reader must have wondered long before this when we would get to the basic factor of talent, so important in the business of acting.

Interestingly, Mr. Slavson reports a high incidence of talent among the children comprising institutional populations.[2] Without going into the reasons therefor, we might say that these conclusions seem to be borne out in the treatment center under discussion here.

It has already been seen in the case of Moody how the discovery of his talent was a result of alert observation. An example of where the talent was much more obvious was that of the boy who played Mr. Bonaparte, the role of an old man whose love for music and his aspiration for his son to become a violinist was second only to his love for Joe, his son. Taking this part was an oversized, overweight, 250-pound boy whose main problem was rooted in the fact that his own father was a dull, inept, avaricious man who could not provide for his children either economically or emotionally. The mother had died when the boy was six. His tendency to clown and joke and play the big "ham," together with his inability to share materially or affectionally with others, made him unpopular in the group. It could be observed, however, that in his very clowning and somewhat egocentric laboriousness, he displayed a rare poise, a sense of hush and pause, and the facility of crescendo while still, in true showmanship style, suggesting reserve power. He also possessed great imagination and resourcefulness. All these are attributes of talent.

His physical hugeness fitted quite well into the creation of a unique, old Italian man. The age of the character presents no special problem in acting. Actually, it is less difficult for adolescents to portray old age than it is for them to act the part of a middle-aged person or that of a character only a few years removed in age from themselves.

If there was divided opinion regarding the effectiveness of other performances, there was unanimous opinion that Mr. Bonaparte truly lived his part. Indeed, in the brief scene when he learns that Joe has been killed in an automobile accident, and the hush of disbelief and astonishment grips Moody, Siggie, Roxy, and Eddie, followed by their general wailing, and when, trembling with fervor, Mr. Bonaparte cuts through the panic with his line, "What did you expect!" and cries real tears as he pounds the table in his grief, one felt that he was expressing his own deep deprivation of the father he was here portraying. This was his moment of full catharsis not only for himself but also for expressing in one line the inevitability and the inexorability of the train of events that led to the final tragedy.

Yet Mr. Bonaparte in spite of his talent would not have been cast on the basis of a reading try-out, as he had serious difficulty in reading. It was interesting that in order to overcome his reading handicap, he was turned over by the director to a fellow staff member who agreed to help him individually with understanding the lines. Within an hour the staff member returned him with the side comment that he couldn't possibly see how this boy could learn the lines, let alone portray the part. Yet of him it was said later, "He has attained insight beyond his years."

On the other hand, there are those whose talent is of a "slick" quality. A case in point is that of our second Siggie, a dark, handsome, curly-haired boy with intense, black eyes. He was a daydreamer who seemed not to hear when spoken to, a boy who was quick to form opinions, and rocklike mute against attempts to be dissuaded. He had wide talents in cartooning and make-up. In acting, too, he showed a great deal of imagination and he was confident and poised on the stage. In the reading try-outs he raced through the lines with glibness and assurance. In a matter of a few days he had learned his lines. But he never got much beyond his first burst of imagination and display of technique. He learned the play too rapidly. As a result, his performance consisted mostly of external techniques, not packed in with emotion and feeling of his own. This was reflected in the gobbling up of his lines, which made it very difficult for him to be understood. He had been in the institution for only three months at the time of his casting, and the director was taken in by his flashiness. Although he gained very little in real insight and understanding from the play, he did feel a part of the group and was eager to engage in further dramatic activity.

Interrelationship Factors

Now that we have considered the importance in casting of the relationship between an actor's personality and that of the character he is to play, we should like to examine another important aspect of casting, namely, the effect of the interrelationships among the individuals comprising the cast to the interrelationships of the characters in the play itself.

We have mentioned, for example, the friendship between our first Moody and Lorna as being a positive factor in helping Moody to become integrated into the group. This sword contained a double edge, however. In the play the character Lorna is loyal to Moody. She exerts pressure on him, in fact, to divorce his wife so that they might get married. In the end, however, she rejects him in favor of Joe. This situation was, in a sense, far too close to reality, for it was our expectation that the affair of this boy and girl too was headed for a break-up and that Moody would be rejected, since their "going steady" was already marked by an "off again, on again" quality. Ordinarily, in casting, it is safer to put some distance between the character and the real-life situation of the person portraying the part. However, our only other choice would have been to cast this boy in the role of Joe, who develops into the real lover of Lorna as the play unfolds, obviously not a worth-while alternative. Besides, it was tempting to see whether the experience of playing out their real-life situation might not help to objectify and resolve it. It was our feeling that such casting would be more therapeutic than the unrealistic wish-fulfillment the role of Joe might have offered this boy.

As a precautionary move, the director faced Moody and Lorna quite frankly with his fear that their personal involvement might jeopardize the progress of the play and that there even existed the danger that one or both of them, in a moment of annoyance or bickering, might walk out on the play entirely. He reminded them that they had broken up a few times already. Both young people assured the director that their individual problem would be subordinated to the interests of the play and that no matter what happened in their relationship, they would "stick it through" to the end.

It was not too long before Moody, appropriately enough,

provoked a discussion around the relationship of the two characters by his asking, "Is the only reason Lorna sticks to Moody that she is sorry for him?"

The director, obviously alert to the implications of this question, thoughtfully countered with the query: "How long does anyone do something for someone out of loyalty or sympathy alone, without getting some satisfaction in return? What was Lorna getting out of this?"

Various points of view emerged. Lorna liked Moody at one time when he was a success and had pulled her out of the depths of despair and, in truth, was beginning to tire of him but was sticking to him out of loyalty. She was getting the "peace and quiet" she claimed she preferred to the excitement and risks of love. The discussion then led into such topics as the difference between loyalty and love, and suddenly the group was involved in a provocative discussion, in general, of problem children and why they came to the institution. The director ventured the suggestion that everyone has problems but wondered how long people can be expected to sustain sympathy for a friend in disaster. How long, for example, would his friends out of loyalty sympathize with a man who has lost his wife? How long would they be solicitous over him, keep having him over for dinner so he would not have to be alone, and so on.

In the resulting discussion, the group gradually brought out the idea that people often cling to their problems long after they have a right to expect extra tolerance for the suffering they have endured, that sometimes they *used* their problems to escape taking responsibility or as an excuse to lean on others. The boy who plays truant from school and then, adopting a helpless look, pleads, "But I am an emotionally disturbed child!" is a good example.

Although the discussion certainly veered from the original topic of the relationship between Lorna and Moody, it is out of such processes that growth takes place. Lorna was quite

moved as she told her case worker with surprise that she
had never thought of love in this way before. "Is it true that
in love you're supposed to *get* something?" she asked in
amazement.

As to whether there was any resolution in the relationship
between Lorna and Moody, we can only report that the final
break did take place during the course of the preparation of
the play. Moody's place in Lorna's affections was taken by
another forlorn sixteen-year-old boy who also had a long
history of failures and had not attended school for two years.
(Her selection of boy friends had a significance of its own.)
Contrary to our expectations, Moody accepted the break
philosophically. There was no hint that he would drop out
of the play. In talking it over with the director, who had
dashed over to see him as he felt guilty that his casting the
two in these roles might possibly have accelerated the break-
up, Moody said: "I admit I feel bad but you don't have to
worry that anything is going to happen. In fact, the way
I feel now, she is gonna have to ask me to make up, not
me her. And even if she does, there is a seventy-five per cent
chance that I wouldn't do it anyway." Such a statement was
a radical departure from his previous pattern of crawling
back to her upon the slightest encouragement.

Moody soon afterward started to make friends with other
girls for the first time. His attitude toward Lorna contained
no particular bitterness. As time went on, he even became
protective toward her. They remained friends, in fact, until
the time of his enlistment in the Navy.

Group Antagonism

An element of the group constellation not given serious
enough consideration was the antagonism of Roxy toward
Mr. Bonaparte, both in their real-life situation and in the
play. The part of Roxy was that of a fight promoter. He was

a man grossly insensitive, crass, blunt, and outspoken. He would never have been able to understand how a fighter could possibly be interested in music.

Roxy, the boy, was slightly built, with sandy hair, who was handicapped in his walking. He had come to the institution because he had thrown a knife at a younger child and had hurt him seriously. Though he was a bright youngster, possessing charm and wit, he was full of bitterness and hate toward the staff who, he insisted, were keeping him in the institution against his will. He compensated for his lack of physical prowess by sarcasm, insolence, and ridicule. He strongly disliked Mr. Bonaparte, his opposite, both physically and temperamentally. There existed as well an element of envy for Mr. Bonaparte, who achieved with his talent where Roxy failed with his brains. The character of Roxy the fight promoter was markedly similar to that of the boy.

When Mr. Bonaparte comes bravely to the fight manager's office to find out "whether the boxing business is good for Joe or not," he is greeted with a sneering "So what!" by Roxy, which was so close to the actor's own way of bullying and sneering at the boy who played Mr. Bonaparte that it could hardly be called sublimation. The play, in a way, provided a sanction for the actor's own original feeling, and the director felt a distressing empathy with the expression, and he submits, in retrospect, that such a sanction should not have been provided. To individuals using this medium for release of such expression drama would be contraindicated. It reminds us of Mr. Slavson's theory in respect to the use of boxing and wrestling as group activities, about which he has the following to say:

. . . They are not sublimations; they are, rather, a controlled—(sometimes not successfully controlled)—acting out of the original wish. . . . The form of expression, and its hidden motives were too close to and reflected too faithfully their unconscious wishes to inflict pain. . . . It seemed to me inadvisable to provide them with a situation in which their latent rage would be activated and its direct expression sanctioned. . . .[3]

Had our roundfaced, roly-poly Tokio played the part of Roxy, such expression of hostility would have been directed at the character of Mr. Bonaparte and not at the actor and would, therefore, have been cathartic without being harmful.

It is, of course, important to keep the entire group constellation in mind when casting for a play. The better the group spirit, the more mutual acceptance existing between the members, the better are the chances for a successful, satisfying achievement for all concerned. Another criterion, therefore, for deciding against an individual's participation in a play production lies in whether the prospective cast member might upset such group morale.

Roxy's attitude toward the play, for instance, was one of indifference. He was pressured into participation by the group. In rehearsals he used subtle devices to provoke giggling and laughing and developed into our greatest discipline problem. It became such a strain that the director finally had to threaten to replace him. Had it not been for his desire not to let the group down, Roxy would have welcomed his release. Not all individuals can benefit from play production at any given time. Certainly one who is basically not interested and not motivated should not be pressured even by the group itself into such an undertaking. In this instance, the indifference could be attributed largely to Roxy's lack of identification with the agency, against which he was in open rebellion. When this is the case, casting is certainly contraindicated. Participation in a drama group requires a certain minimum of social consciousness without which the sustained effort and co-operation with the group will not be forthcoming. The wise director will wait until such a condition exists rather than risk the adverse effect upon the group and upon the production that the casting of such a person would be likely to entail, even though from an audience point of view he might be successful, which was the case with Roxy.

Strengthening Group Spirit

There are times when a director casts with an eye toward strengthening the group. The major characteristics of the group in our first cast were those of the neurotic and the withdrawn, whose main interests were intellectual and cultural. There was, already, a strong subgroup led by Joe and including Eddie and Tokio. On the fringes, too, were Roxy and to a lesser extent Siggie. Moody's primary allegiance, as mentioned before, was to Lorna. Thus we see that there was a cohesiveness to this group.

The second cast, under the leadership of Joe, was made up more of boys with active interests, who were more popular as a group on the campus. Within the group itself, however, there were no such strong subgroups as described in the first cast. Focusing on individual needs, in consultation with case workers, the director had cast isolates in the new parts. Already discussed have been Tokio, the boy needing release of hostility, and Siggie, the daydreamer with the flashy talent. Another isolate was Carp, a boy who constantly sought attention, who asked a question a minute, and who could always be counted upon to interrupt an absorbing moment in directing by a tap on the arm to ask what time it was. Moody II had, in a way, grown out of the group, as he was working full time in preparation for his discharge and already, in a sense, had one foot out of the institution. But he was the most reliable cast member.

In order to bolster the group the director cast in the part of Driscoll a thirteen-year-old boy who begged for a chance to be in the play, no matter how small a part it was. He was an obsessive-compulsive neurotic boy, plagued by fears of disease. But he was one of the most genuinely liked boys on the campus because he so thoroughly identified with the group and enjoyed group living. Though the director could not locate even microscopically some talent for acting nor find within his own imagination the spark with which to create out of this boy the slightest resemblance to a fight investigator, nevertheless a calculated risk was taken with this part, consisting in all of four lines, one minute on stage. The boy was a great help in building group spirit and co-operation, not as a leader but as a good follower. It was interesting to note how seriously he took his part. Of course, it was always our stress that there are no small parts, only small players. He seemed to get a real thrill and a sense of adventure out of all the back-stage excitement, even to having make-up applied. Moreover, he performed beyond our expectations and felt himself quite successful.

Another step taken by the director in creating a group bond was to add to the cast a bodyguard for Eddie, consisting of two boys (to the consternation of our costumer and make-up man, who now needed to find two more hats and overcoats and handle an increased make-up chore) who were leaders on the campus and had good relationships with Joe, Mr. Bonaparte, Driscoll, Roxy, and others. They were eager to be identified with the production but were too reticent about taking on any speaking roles. Their participation helped to create a more enthusiastic spirit within the group, and the entire cast felt a certain alliance with the director in being a part of this ingenious contrivance.

Summarizing these experiences, we would conclude that in casting for parts in a play, a director would need to consider the following factors:

1. The emotional effect produced upon the director.
2. The basic talent possessed. This would include such faculties as sense of mimicry, timing, suspense, build-up, cre-

scendo, pause, stage presence and poise, the courage to "give," to put oneself completely into a role.

3. The intensity of the individual's desire for the part and his interest in the activity.

4. The existing potentials for understanding the ideas of the play and the behavior of the character.

5. The relationship of the actor's to the character's personality traits.

6. The emotional needs of the moment.

7. The group factors and interrelationships.

8. Technical considerations. These would include pleasing contrasts in voice, awareness of unnecessary physical distractions, or incongruous combinations such as an overly tall girl playing opposite a short boy in the roles of lovers.

FOOTNOTES

1. *See* Chapter Two, p. 33.

2. *See* S. R. Slavson, *Re-educating the Delinquent* (New York: Harper & Brothers, 1954), p. 124.

3. *Ibid.*, p. 112.

CHAPTER NINE

Benefits of Participation in Play Production

IN THE NEXT TWO CHAPTERS we should like to summarize the benefits to the individual and the group of participation in play production and the features of this programming which lend themselves to such achievements. We have already taken up in detail two play productions, including the skills and techniques employed and the value to certain individuals taking part. We do not conceive of the skills and methods demonstrated as applying to only the settings described herein but rather as generic in nature and universally applicable. Ego building, enrichment of living, mental hygiene, emotional and social growth are objectives of schools, church organizations, community centers, little theatre groups, as well as to treatment centers and mental hospitals.

Acceptance of Self and Others

It has been seen how the creative approach in play direction is a process not only of finding the positives in an individual's make-up and thereby building ego, but of sometimes turning liabilities into assets. Mr. Bonaparte's hugeness, Moody's irritability, Scrooge's wiriness, and our second Joe's "Huh!" are but a few examples of how the individual can gain the feeling that what he is and what he thinks and says is important and worth while. It is amusing to reflect on our second Carp, the pesty boy, who threw his arms around the director after the play was over and exclaimed, "Boy, was this ego building for me!" (Children in treatment centers pick up the social work terminology distressingly fast.) His same bespectacled, studious demeanor which had always brought him ridicule and rejection were particularly suited to the role of Carp and now brought him recognition from the audience and a greater acceptance from the group. It bears out our point of view that generally it is better to assign roles suited to one's appearance, personality, and temperament, because such casting starts with the premise of accepting a person as he is.

It is a maxim in education and mental hygiene that before one can respect others, he must first respect himself. The illustrations are replete with examples of children who had lost confidence in themselves and had suffered many failures. For one like Moody, his participation in the play gave him his first success, with the result that he gained confidence in himself and consequently was able to move on to wider social relationships.

It is a great thrill and satisfaction when the result of a creative endeavor is shown to an audience, for it is out of such display that recognition and status are gained. In the play "Golden Boy" every member of the cast gained some recognition because of his being in the play.

Within the group itself, the friendship between Joe, Eddie, Tokio was cemented and enhanced. They developed an especially amiable feeling toward one another, and while they have all been discharged, they still correspond with one another as well as with Roxy. Indeed, Joe, Moody, Lorna, and Mr. Bonaparte, especially, were regarded with a new respect among all the children on the campus and were certainly so regarded by the members of the cast.

The Release of Emotions

Drama provides an excellent medium for the release of emotions. A good example of how such a release was obtained occurred in the winter of 1948 in a community center setting. This involved a college sophomore who had joined the drama group because of a broad interest in the arts and a special interest in painting and scene design. He was a person with intellectual interests. He was logical, methodical, disputatious. Though he had a discriminating sense of humor, his laugh was inward. He talked in what might be called a cultured tone, but his enunciation was indistinct, his words being gobbled up in his throat and nose.

He mentioned, in casual conversation with the director, that one of his difficulties was that he could not express either anger or affection, not even to his immediate family. This caused him some misgivings.

When the group decided to do an excerpt from the play "Winterset" for an opening-of-the-season party, this boy asked if he could do the part of Mio. He had "fallen in love" with the role and felt confident he could do it. The character Mio was a person with a mission—to avenge the murder of his father—and as such was filled with bitterness and anger. Our would-be actor had never expressed anything close to such emotions. Besides, he had not yet had any acting experience.

After a long period of hesitation on the director's part, and pleading on the part of the boy, he was finally given the role. It was felt that his own desire here should enable him to succeed. As has been discussed already, the person's own desire is a valid factor in casting.

There was long and hard work. The boy threw himself completely into the task. He practiced swearing at the director; he threw things around the auditorium. With the director's help, he worked ceaselessly on his articulation. Every conceivable variety of movement to go with the lines was brought out to facilitate his expression.

The performance was creditable. The attention of the audience was held most of the time and the meanings of the lines were projected intelligibly. What is most important, however, is that the boy himself had a feeling of successful accomplishment. He gleefully reported following this experience that he suddenly found himself freer on the give-and-take at home. The week following the play this same lad attended a large midwestern conference at which, for the first time in his life, he had enough confidence in his verbal ability to get up and speak from the floor to a large audience.

This is an instance where casting a part according to the opposite qualities of a person did prove beneficial. The significant factor here, however, is that the person himself really wanted to try it, proving perhaps that he was ready for such an experience. There is also the factor that the character Mio's resentments were really overlaid on an essentially poetic, philosophical, and sensitive spirit, qualities which our actor did possess in common with Mio.

The girl who played the role of Lorna in "Golden Boy" is an example of one who obtained a catharsis through her portrayal of the role. She was a tall, slender, stately-looking girl of sixteen, who was endowed with everything—looks, talents, and intelligence. Her IQ was in the 140's. However, her endowments brought her only anguish. Her parents, people of average ability, feared her brightness, and the mother stated frankly that she would have been more comfortable with a child who was not so much above them. The mother's rejection took the form of constant criticism. If the girl came home from school with all A's, she was greeted with the recrimination that she had forgotten to do her chores that day. She finally came to the institution because she had stolen a car and was unmanageable. There was an impenetrable veneer about her. She rarely showed anger and had never shed tears. Nevertheless, an air of sadness surrounded her. In her friendships she seemed to seek out the lowly and the forlorn. It was a matter of constant amazement to the staff to observe her open affection for Moody, with his contrasting dearth of abilities. Subsequently, her other boy friends followed the same pattern.

During the course of the rehearsals her attitude toward the character of Lorna was in a constant state of flux. At one time she sympathized with her plight; at another she condemned her treatment of Joe. She turned in the most polished performance of the cast. She was a valuable asset to the production because she could sustain the role. From an artistic point of view she was compared favorably with a professional actress of a local little theatre performance a few years back. It was interesting to note that her own lack of affect fitted in rather well with the character of Lorna, who had developed a hard crust over her feelings throughout her years of association with boxing managers, promoters, and the like.

One of the threads of the play was the developing love between Joe and Lorna, the climax of which is reached in a scene where he finally pierces through the crust. Lorna breaks down in this scene and cries when she tries to maintain that what she wants is "peace and quiet, not love." In the first performance it was a sign of some interest that she could show some emotion, as her lack of affect caused the staff considerable concern. In the repeat performance, this was one of the most moving scenes of the play as she shed real tears. Reports from the case worker revealed that the "peace and quiet" she sought was in direct reaction to the tumult of her own home. The tears that she shed were not only for the plight of Lorna the character but were the pouring-out of her own life's anguish.

In addition to the direct expression of emotion experienced in a portrayal of a part, the aspect of rehearsing in which discussions and analyses of the play take place very often also helps bring strong feelings into the open.

A good example of how feelings were stimulated through such discussion occurred at a rehearsal of a one-act play, "Jacob Comes Home," again at a community center drama group. This play dealt with the persecution of the Jews in Germany under Hitler's regime. Under discussion was the character of Hulda, a middle-aged Jewish woman, frightened, restless, always wanting to go home because her "children were alone in the house." One of the questions put to the group was, "What kind of a person do you suppose Hulda was a few years back, before Hitler came into power?"

Among some of the answers received was one which imagined her to be a person who tried to hush up her Jewishness. As the discussion began to develop some consensus around this interpretation, a Jewish high school senior girl, somewhat timid, shy and reserved, took exception to the general opinion that Jews should not hide their Jewishness. With a good deal of feeling, she said that she herself didn't like most of the Jewish girls in her classes in high school because they were loud-mouthed and uncouth. The way they acted reflected upon her and she resented it. She thought that Jews had to be especially careful about their manner and not go around advertising their Jewishness, since they were especially susceptible to criticism. This surprising outburst led to a general discussion of anti-Semitism, a discussion which occupied the rest of the rehearsal period.

Just how much the discussion helped to clarify the girl's self-hatred is difficult to tell. It is known, however, that she did become one of the nuclei of this group in the next few years and went out to undertake volunteer work in other Jewish agencies.

Distinguishing Between the Real and the Imaginary

Closely related to the release of emotion is the release of fantasy. Slavson has described art as "mediated reality." [1] Expression of fantasy through the controlled medium of dramatic art distinguishes it from reality, establishes a clear line of demarcation between the one and the other. The more the play is geared to reality, the clearer the issues involved, the more believable the characters and the situations, the better can the art form accomplish its distinguishing function between reality and fantasy.

A case in point here would be that of the boy who played Eddie Fuseli, the racketeer. Our boy Eddie was sixteen years old and had only in the past year brought himself out of a withdrawn, schizoid state in which he had been immersed for many years. In recent months he had been preoccupied with murder mysteries and gangster stories. It was he, it will be remembered, who wrote the "Dragnet"-type skit which started the interest in play production in the treatment center. The character of Eddie Fuseli was also that of a gangster. Under the circumstances, it was decided to have this boy play the role, especially since it was the part he wanted. He performed quite creditably. The effect of his experience seemed to be that he had gotten the gangster fantasy out of his system. At least we noticed no further manifestations of this preoccupation.

Enrichment of Living

The great prevalence of television and movies in the recreation diet of our children makes it highly desirable for them to develop a sense of discrimination and selection, if they are not to be swallowed up by the pervasive passivity of constantly being entertained and if they are not to be fashioned to the mediocrity that dominates these mass media. That passivity has become a wide concern is pointed up by the emergence of the field of recreation in which much is being done to counteract the paralyzing effects of spectatorism. The great revival of interest and participation in folk and square dancing, as well as the constant growing interest in Little Theatre, shows that people basically prefer active participation to passive observation.

The very experience of play producing itself arouses powers of observation and imagination which develop a critical facility for appreciating movies and plays. The cast discussion around the Goodyear Playhouse television program, already covered in detail in Chapter Six, is an example of a purposefully designed experience in the development of such appreciation and taste. There were evidences of the success of this venture as several boys kidded the director afterward with his having ruined their complacent enjoyment of the run-of-the-mill television and movie programs. They suddenly found themselves looking at both the plot and the technical aspects of acting with a much more critical eye.

It has undoubtedly already become apparent what a vast amount of skill can be gained from a dramatic production. Increasing knowledge and skill enriches life. Skills in communication, in organization, in business management, in all the various crafts are constantly being developed.

Brain Food

Contact with good plays introduces us to places and people different from ourselves, yet containing the element of universality in which we all can find identification. Constant probing into ideas and themes begins to develop in the participants a philosophy of life. Interests broaden and expand. Social responsibility, then, broadens and expands. A value system begins to be implanted. A rehearsal period in a theatre group seldom ends without stopping for coffee afterward, where heated discussions take place on all phases of life and world affairs.

We have already seen in what detail such ideas as love, greed, money, or psychology, were examined in "A Christmas Carol." In analyzing the play "Golden Boy," too, such ideas as love, boxing, power, music, loyalty, were bandied around by the cast as an integral process of producing the play. The reader has already seen a few examples of such discussions. Quite revealing to the adolescents was the deglamorization of the boxing business. Joe's line in which he says he doesn't like his manager because "I'm just a silver mine for him. He treats me like a possession. He bangs me around with a shovel . . ." became more and more significant as we dug into the meaning.

Our adolescents have fondly labeled such discussions as "brain food." There are those who believe that adolescents prefer plays that deal with situations on their own level and characters of their own age.[2] This is an underestimation of the adolescent's interests. It is our experience that the older adolescents especially can be stimulated by broader themes. To be sure, they will draw from them applications to their own situations. Actually, we have found that the best "lead in" to the discussion of an adolescent group problem is to start with something broad and general. For example, the way one might talk to a group of adolescents about their sloppiness and disorder is to approach these matters philosophically through a discussion in general of the topic, "Respect." He might talk to delinquents about their code of not wanting to be known as "chicken" by going at it through a broad discussion of "Courage." He could talk to them about sex by starting the discussion with "The Nature of Man."

A good illustration of the adolescent's interest in broader subjects was brought to the writer's attention just recently by Joe II, who suggested that it would be worth while to tackle the play, "Julius Caesar," because Mark Anthony's speech contained such good psychology.

Understanding Ourselves and Others

A unique aspect of play production is its focus on human behavior. The great amount of knowledge gained about the animal man and his actions and reactions is certainly evident from our illustrations. For example, let us turn to a discussion with Joe Bonaparte regarding his speech that goes as follows:

> "With music I am never alone when I am alone—playing music. That's like saying 'I am man. I belong here. How do you do, world. Good evening.' When I play music nothing is closed to me. I am not afraid of people and what they say. There is no war in music. It's not like the streets. Does this sound funny?"

Joe was concerned about his ability to give this speech naturally. After clarifying the meanings of the lines, Joe saw that the character was quite sensitive. The director asked him what kind of neighborhood he supposed Joe lived in. Joe replied, "Where there is a great deal of fighting on the streets and stuff like that," to which the director added, "and wrangling and bickering and quarreling." In further discussion of this aspect of living, Joe became fascinated with the paradox between the character who reacted to violence, harshness, and bitterness by withdrawing to music, yet at the same time chose to go into the profession of boxing where violence is the chief stock in trade.

Later Joe and the director went over another scene in which Joe had already achieved success in the boxing game. In this scene, he was expressing his feeling that he was not sure he liked the success and that he still had not found peace and contentment. In going over the scene and considering how it could be expressed, the director asked whether Joe had ever anticipated some good time like a trip or a party and then found it did not measure up to his expectations. He answered that not only had that happened to him often but it seemed to him it happened to everyone. The director summed up for Joe that good drama does universalize through the characters and their problems the experiences that many people face.

The production of a play is a process of experimentation and analysis. Since the person himself is the object of constant evaluation and since the person is creating a character from the base of his own personality, this medium presents, therefore, the opportunity to inculcate in the actors the facility for looking at themselves objectively. It becomes legitimate to inquire into motives, into mechanisms, into the whys of a character's behavior.

We hasten to point out again that such discussion is only in terms of the character and not of the person. To investigate the motives of the person himself is the area of therapy. Discovering the mechanisms and the rationale of a character's behavior can *stimulate* the actor to examine his own experiences objectively. But it is not within the legitimate purposes of creative play directing to encourage the discussion of these experiences with the director. A person's own experiences are his own business. When Shelley Winters, a member of the Actors' Studio, a school for "Method" acting, was asked, for example, what experiences in her own life did she recall to summon up tears for "A Place in the Sun," she replied, "If I told you, and you printed it, I would sue you." [3]

On the other hand, inquiry into what a character's experiences might have been is pertinent to the successful portrayal of the character. We try out an action. We then talk about it. What could be done to make it more convincing, more lifelike? What is the reason for this behavior? Why does the character act one way toward one person and differently toward another? Objectivity comes from the knowledge that whatever is said cannot be taken as a personal reference. We are talking about the character. What is important is the success of the play. The director is impersonal, focusing on the character rather than on the actor as a person. He even refers to individuals by the name of the character they are portraying, thus further contributing to the impartiality of his analyses.

Discussion of characters develops understanding. There are no all blacks or all whites. Behavior has logic and reason, and is purposeful. As we trace the circumstances leading to an action, no matter how irritating or shocking it be, we begin to see such action not as a result of some inherent inner bestiality in the character but as something arising almost inevitably out of the chain of events. A true test of a good play or movie is when the audience comes away with the feeling that none of the characters could have behaved in any other way than they did. When the Fates bring together a protagonist (Macbeth) behaving in a manner which is logical, reasonable, inevitable for him, and an antagonist (Macduff) behaving in a manner which is logical, reasonable, and inevitable for him, a conflict which "tears one to pieces" is produced. This is produced precisely because in understanding the circumstances and motivations leading to Macbeth's behavior, we begin to sympathize with him.

It is a highly debatable point, of course, whether a person will apply to himself what he learns about a character. Students of human behavior are well aware of the mechanism of projection by which, all too often, we see our own faults in others. Wilson and Ryland say, however, in discussing dramatics as an element of program content:

> The members usually begin by commenting on the characters in the play. Gradually they relate various factors in the play to their own lives. They usually talk more freely in the group setting than in individual conferences with the worker. By exchanging ideas within the group they discover that others have the same feelings and problems, and they learn with relief that they are not unusual or 'queer.' [4]

We might say, without going far afield, that individuals will at least relate to their own lives such factors which are not, or which they may come to see will not be, threatening to them. It would be most valuable, it seems, to explore the possibilities of how the factor of sympathy gained for a character might be the avenue through which the individual will begin to apply to himself what he learns about a character, especially since he uses himself to create the character in the first place. When it does become too threatening to an individual to make such an application, to expose himself to himself, drama always allows him the refuge of the character.

We could say with reasonable certainty that there was at least a great deal of activity in "pecking away" at insight. In speaking to Joe, for instance, about his music speech, the director picked out a few of the head-scratching and neck-clutching grimaces Joe was making and showed him that this speech was intended to be delivered with precisely the embarrassment these movements seemed to portray. In order to make this point clearer, the director then asked Joe whether he had ever wanted to do something that he hated to admit to anyone. In keeping with the principle of staying out of the area of therapy, Joe was told he need not answer this question directly but should think about it and put himself in the same situation here. Then the director turned the question around and asked whether Joe had ever done things that he really did not want to do but felt impelled to do because others were doing them. While Joe smiled acquiescently, the director ventured the suggestion that he had gotten into some of his difficulties such as car stealing in precisely this manner. Joe admitted that this had been one of the major factors in his delinquencies. After this discussion, Joe seemed able to absorb the speech much more comfortably. The mention of car stealing was justified in this instance only because the director was personally involved in uncovering the incident. Of course, this was an individual not a group rehearsal.

There was some evidence that this type of constant probing had an effect on Joe's daily life and resulted in some insight into human behavior in general, if not insight into himself. At one of the cottage self-government meetings held shortly after the production of the play, for instance, one of the most withdrawn, compulsive boys was the subject of complaint by the group because of his failure to carry out his chores. A new cottage father had already jumped to his feet to protect the boy, but it was unnecessary. Joe, the same boy who earlier had not been able to see why everyone was not punished alike for the same offense, now calmly stood up and explained that this boy could not be looked upon as any other who might have done the same thing. He argued that this boy's problem was precisely that he could not get up on time, so how could he be expected to get the dining-room table set on time? He suggested that this boy should not be assigned to such a duty, and that in the long run he could not come within the scope or pattern of group rules and regulations. This recommendation was met with complete agreement on the part of the other boys.

There was also some evidence that this type of character-probing activity was reflected in social case work contacts. As has already been mentioned, Joe finally began to talk with his case worker about his parents and about his own reaction patterns. Lorna, too, brought to her case worker her concern about any possible significance in her inability to express emotion. She associated the character of Lorna with herself in this respect.

It was stated by the superintendent of the institution in regard to "Golden Boy," "One might well say that almost every child came out of this play in a somewhat more treatable manner, so that the play worked as a catalytic agent. It was one of the real meaningful experiences to the children in terms of their own capacities and problems, which were partly reflected in the play."

Earning Success

> The law of nature is that a certain amount of work is neces-
> sary to produce a certain quality of good. If you want knowl-
> edge you must toil for it; if food, you must toil for it; if pleas-
> ure, you must toil for it.
>
> JOHN RUSKIN

Although there has been constant stress throughout this
book on the value of success, we have also tried to make it
clear that success does not come cheaply. Success becomes
meaningful in proportion to the effort that has been invested,
the challenge which has been met, the vicissitudes which
have been borne, and the frustrations which have been overcome. Certainly, it requires a high degree of judgment on the
part of the director to ascertain whether his charges are ready
to undertake such a challenge. But, on the other hand, the
inner rewards and satisfactions gained are as great as the
struggle invested. Who has forgotten his first part in a play?
The experiences of many of the individuals who took part
in "A Christmas Carol" and "Golden Boy" will be for them,
we are sure, a fond memory lasting all their lives.

It has been said that there is a tendency on the part of our
depression-raised parents to compensate for their own childhood deprivations by making of their children a catch-all for
their well-intentioned, perhaps, but misguided overgenerosity.
With its focus as much as it has been on the problems of
the underprivileged child, society is now becoming aware of
the problems of the overprivileged child, arising from our
prosperity-ridden middle-class families. In her thoughtful article, "No Man Is an Island," Agnes Meyer points to the
pseudoquality of our present-day peace and prosperity, as-
serting that underneath it all there is a great dissatisfaction,
an "underlying melancholy." [5] In too many cases their children's lives are made up of pseudosuccesses, in which they
are constantly getting much more than they give. Just as

people want activity in which they can participate rather than merely observe, so do they want their successes to be earned. It was the experience in forming the drama group in the treatment institution that it filled the need of children to put forth the goods for value received. This was evidenced in their rejection of any scheme for money raising which would be "donation" tinged.

Not only the play production as a whole but each process in its preparation is an experience in overcoming obstacles. The submission to objective criticism gives the participants conditioning to face their flaws without becoming overwhelmed, to meet the challenge by increased effort rather than discouragement and, perhaps what is most important, to know that when praise does come it is genuine and not gratuitous.

Satisfying the Need for Adventure

The desire of young people for challenge and excitement brings us to another benefit of participation in play production, that of satisfying the need for adventure. A play project with its back-stage tensions and anticipation, the thrill of waiting to come on stage at precisely the right moment with the telephone ring, watching the cues, seeing one's self in make-up—all help to fulfill this need. Even more so does the necessity for staying up late at times, the decision to send out for sandwiches, the need to solicit hats for the costumer, and the many emergencies which one comes to expect, such as the last minute blow-out of a fuse. Going out afterward, the meeting of minds to solve grave problems in production—lighting, signaling, cueing—all form outlets for the spirit of adventure. Indeed, the creation of a character is in and of itself exciting. With the use of the creative approach in acting, there is the thrill of making something of one's own. There is the suspense of working at it to see where it leads and the thrill of accomplishment when it turns out well.

FOOTNOTES

1. S. R. Slavson, *Re-educating the Delinquent* (New York: Harper & Brothers, 1954), p. 125.

2. S. R. Slavson, *Creative Group Education* (New York: Association Press, 1938), p. 115.

3. Seymour Peck, "The Temple of 'The Method,'" *The New York Times Magazine*, May 6, 1956, Section 6, Part I, p. 47.

4. Gertrude Wilson and Gladys Ryland, *Social Group Work Practice* (Boston: Houghton Mifflin Company, 1949), p. 300. By permission of the publisher.

5. Agnes E. Meyer, "No Man Is an Island," *Social Work*, Vol. I, No. 3, July 1956, p. 3.

CHAPTER TEN

Features Favorable to Personal and Social Growth

IN THE PRECEDING CHAPTER we attempted to list specific educational, social, and emotional benefits that can be derived from participation in a play. In this chapter we should like to summarize the features of the medium of play production which lend themselves favorably to the attainment of these benefits.

Highly Individual, Highly Social

No activity of the school is more communal in its nature, or more diversified in the talents used, than is dramatic art.[1]

Since the aim of good human relations and modern education is to fulfill individual needs, a medium which contains ample opportunity to utilize individual talents and capabilities would be considered highly valuable. Out of a dramatic production innumerable activities radiate which enable the individuals, with the director's help, to find some phase of the production in which they can participate and to which they can contribute. Among such activities might be listed painting, designing, make-up, building, sewing, advertising, ticket selling, publicity. And if there are those who have none of the skills needed in the above operations, there are other jobs such as curtain pulling, collecting properties, handing out programs, arranging, organizing, setting up refreshment concessions, and a host of others in which they can find a place.

Although there exist ample related activities to occupy anyone who cares to be so involved, it is true, however, that most of the members of dramatic groups are primarily interested in an opportunity to act. Here, too, no one need be excluded. For we all have the basic equipment necessary for acting—a body, a voice, a personality. From the standpoint of individual capacity, it is this writer's belief that any person who wants to can be helped to accomplish a creditable portrayal of a role on the stage. As Sybil Thorndike says, "Acting is the art which is common to all of us (everybody can act—more or less!)." [2]

As far as diverse types of people are concerned, all can be utilized in play production. In both plays used as illustrations in this book there were such extreme types as the incongruously large and the uncommonly thin, the attractive and the peculiar looking, the physically handicapped and the athletic, the very bright and the dull, the normal and the extremely disturbed. The most important factor is that the casts included many whose first chance for success and participation in a group activity was in the play.

There may be a question, however, in the mind of the reader. After all, are there not limitations to the medium of play production as to the number of people who can be assigned parts for any one play that might be in production at any one time?

Some years ago, when the writer was co-director of a theatre group of adolescents and young adults at a community center, this was, indeed, a problem with which we were faced.

In looking back over the few years of this group's existence, we found a certain pattern recurring: Every year there were try-outs for a major production. More people tried out, however, than there were parts available. Despite efforts to interest those not receiving roles to participate in some of the related activities, most did not appear again until the next time there were try-outs. It occurred to us that here was a wide, unmet need. To meet this need, we expanded the group to include a mobile theatre. The writer's colleague continued to direct the major productions for which tickets were sold to the general public. The writer, on the other hand, undertook to direct one-act plays and skits with those not cast for parts and having little or no experience. These skits were taken around to other organizations and performed for their various affairs.

In this way, many people who had been on the periphery of the group were now brought in and were able to gain the outlet they sought, as well as to find social satisfactions. Included in this group were three girls who subsequently revealed that they had been unable to get parts in their high school plays where those who had experience and more obvious talent were usually chosen. Among others drawn into this group were a young adult man and wife who were frightened of appearing before an audience. They undertook to be responsible for properties. They attended many rehearsals and enjoyed listening to and sometimes participating in the discussions. Finally, at a cast party, the wife did read a parody for the group and the husband participated in charades.

Another young professional woman also did not feel secure enough to act but attended rehearsals. She said she enjoyed just watching. When time for performance drew near, she volunteered to do stage duties.

One young adolescent boy, a junior in high school, got satisfaction just out of pulling the curtain. His enthusiasm for this job was always a source of great amusement. He would stick his head out on the proscenium, concerned whether the curtain pulling had come off properly. The director made sure to include in his notes to the cast some comment, positive or negative, about the curtain. (Pulling the curtain *is* important. Pulled sloppily or jerkily, it can break the illusion of the play.)

There are some limitations, however, which should be mentioned, particularly at the adolescent and young adult levels. In our experience, by far the majority of those turning out for try-outs seemed to be women. Yet most good plays seem to have more men parts than women. Because of this disparity we found that often we were unable to involve all of the girls, while some of the men had to do double duty. The reason for such disparity may be because of the aura of femininity with which drama has been associated. It may be due, perhaps, to the very artificiality of the external techniques which, to a healthy growing boy, appear to be, in the vernacular, "sissified" and not in keeping with "red-blooded" qualities of manliness. Or it may be due to the simple fact that in our culture men have many more opportunities for emotional outlets than do women. Whatever the reason, this is a factor which must be considered when developing a dramatics program.

It may be noted that in the second performance of "Golden Boy" there was method to the director's madness in encouraging the manly boys' participation, for this helped to establish drama as a high prestige program.

Not only is drama highly individual, allowing one to find his own individual place within this medium, according to his own skills, capacities, and personality dispositions, but drama is also extremely social or, to refer to the quotation at the beginning of this chapter, "communal in its nature." Since man strives to be an independent individual with his own specific, self-assertive aspirations, he at the same time is a social being, depending on others for many of his satisfactions.[3]

The production of a play is essentially a co-operative undertaking. The actor must depend and rely on the person in charge of properties, the make-up man, the costumer, the sound effects man and so on if he is to have success. The scenery must be co-ordinated with lights. An actor missing a rehearsal disrupts all the plans and organization and incurs the resentment of his colleagues. In "Golden Boy," for example, a replacement was necessary for the first Anna because of her constant tardiness at rehearsals. The group found this behavior so annoying and resentments reached such a pitch that the director felt it necessary to take this action.

On the other hand, an example of how the group's interaction with an individual can change the attitude toward him from rejection to mutual acceptance, was illustrated in the case of the first Carp. He was a fifteen-year-old boy who had been in the institution for six years. In all that time he had never engaged in a group activity, felt contempt for his peers, and did not know how to share. He had undertaken individual enterprises in woodwork and had periods in which he was helpful to his cottage mother in decorating, since he had great skill with his hands and possessed a keen mechanical sense, but always worked alone, never with the group. He was regarded by the group as a grouch.

He was quite a compulsive, stubborn boy who could not be pried off his own pace. He was very short in stature, standing an even five feet in height, and was quite sensitive about his size. Any slight affront to his dignity was cause for a torrent of profanity and hateful invective. One might gather that this boy had been a neglect case, coming from a home in which he had been subjected to merciless beatings.

Not only did he play the part of Carp, a "street corner" philosopher who was a neighbor to Mr. Bonaparte, but he was also the technical manager, having the responsibility for lighting and properties and cast photographs. As the play reached the phase in which final rehearsals kept the cast working late at night during the summer heat, he took it upon himself to prepare lemonade and snacks for everyone. Although his method of distribution was somewhat highhanded, his consideration was still greatly appreciated and gave the cast a feeling that basically he did want to co-operate.

He began to be accepted, first in a tone of amusement. The feeling then began to emerge that Carp had to be accepted as he was—cranky, set in his own ways—but if one were patient enough with him, he could be relied upon to have everything ready back-stage.

Boy-Girl Relationships

Another important feature which should be mentioned here is the outlet for wholesome boy-girl relationships provided by a dramatic project. Co-ed programming of teen-agers is often quite difficult not only because of the diverse interests but because of the feeling of awkwardness with the opposite sex that exists at this age. The play brings them together under circumstances in which all have something specific to do in contrast to the canteen-type of lounge in which there is a great deal of embarrassed shuffling about. Mutual respect is here obtained for qualities other than looks and dancing.

Competition Minimized

The problem of undesirable competition is also one with which social workers and modern educators are concerned. According to Slavson, undesirable competition would be defined as the "act of seeking or endeavoring to gain what another is endeavoring to gain at the same time." [4]

The problem is well expressed by the noted leader in the field of recreation, E. O. Harbin, in his very useful book, *The Fun Encyclopedia:*

> . . . There is a feeling among a considerable number of educators and other persons interested in human welfare that the importance of competition as a factor in play has been considerably overemphasized. Some even go so far as to charge that highly organized competitive programs are deterrents to the

emergence of proper social attitudes. They insist that there should be larger use made of co-operative activities. . . .[5]

The difficulty with activities stressing competitiveness is that for every winner, there must be a loser. There are those who may argue that losing is life and one must become hardened to experiencing failures in order to face those inevitable in the future. Unfortunately, it does not work that way. It is only when one has had the security of successes that he is better able to meet failure when it comes. Unless one has great strength, losing robs one of confidence and self-respect, leads to further failures, further inhibits the capacity to grow and to gain satisfactions, and develops further inferiority feelings. In regard to inferiority feelings, Wendell Johnson states:

> There is an old saying that nothing fails like failure. . . . The tears which it produces water the soil from which it grows ever more luxuriantly.[6]

It is inherent in a mental hygiene approach of working with people to build on strengths rather than play on weaknesses, to discover where one can best use his capacities to achieve successes rather than being subjected to unnecessary failures.

Everybody who participates in a dramatic production can win. The winning, in fact, often depends on how well, not on how poorly, others are contributing to the total project. In using the creative approach, especially, the emphasis is on the idea that there are "no small parts, only small players"; there are no stars, but each character is his own unique creation. This philosophy comes directly from the Stanislavski school of acting, where the performance of even such an important group as the Moscow Art Theatre Players drew the following comment in *The New York Herald Tribune*:

> . . . There were no individuals in The Cherry Orchard or The Lower Depths as the Moscow players brought these plays to life before one's eyes. Or, perhaps, it would be more accu-

rate to say that every character was an individual. At any rate there were no leading men or women, and the memory that one took from the experience was a totality. . . .[7]

Project-Type Program

One of the characteristics of a good group is stated by Harleigh Trecker to be as follows:

> . . . the group work group must have some degree of cohesiveness, some bond that will hold the members of the group together for at least a minimum period of time. . . . Whatever it may be, the group must have a reasonable expectancy of remaining together for a sufficient period of time to achieve its objectives.[8]

The value of projects is also recognized in modern education. The noted educator William Heard Kilpatrick calls a project purposeful activity or the hearty purposeful act. This act is the typical unit of the worthy life.[9] Satisfactory living consists in having worth-while things to do, not just aimless dawdling or drifting. We don't just walk—we walk somewhere (unless we decide to take a walk for recreation, in which case this becomes the purpose). We don't just build—we build something. Kilpatrick goes on to say:

> The richness of life is seen upon reflection to depend, in large measure at least, upon the tendency of what one does to suggest and prepare for succeeding activities. Any activity—beyond the barest physical want—which does not thus "lead on" becomes in time stale and flat. . . .[10]

> Wholehearted purposeful activity in a social situation is the best guarantee of the utilization of the child's native capacities now too frequently wasted. Under proper guidance purpose means efficiency, not only in reaching the projected end of the activity itself, but even more in securing from the activity the learning which it potentially contains.[11]

A dramatic production is a wholehearted purposeful activity, lending cohesiveness around a goal, insuring continuation of interest and activity.

Intergroup and Community Relations Cemented

One of the criteria by which we judge the success of social group work is in the degree to which the group matures in its sense of responsibility to the agency, to the degree to which it participates in community and agency events.[12]

The fact that the results of a creative effort are displayed to an audience is a highly important feature of the program medium of drama. Not only does it provide opportunities for status and recognition of the drama group, but the wider organization of which it is a part also gains a sense of pride in its theatre group and enjoys reflected glory from its achievements. In the treatment center the effect on the campus was noticeable.

One of the evidences of such wide group bond was in the reaction of the youngest age group, seven-to-ten-year-olds. It had been decided not to encourage their attendance at the performances because of the serious content of the play and because of our fear that they might disrupt the performance. In order not to single them out, it was decided to charge twenty-five cents admission for children, confident they would not want to pay the price. To everyone's complete surprise, they not only insisted on paying their quarters and being granted admission, but, as described previously, hung on every word of the actors. It was felt that they had identified with the project and felt a sense of belonging in participating as an audience.

Some of this feeling had been generated throughout the campus by a pre-performance advertisement of the play wherein each of the cast members had an opportunity to give his favorite line from the play and a short excerpt was also presented. This took place at one of the daily flag-raising programs, a traditional summer program activity at this institution. It was one of the most successful flag-raising activities that summer.

The campus-wide spirit was also evidenced in the many children who began asking to join the drama club. As far as the children were concerned, the full-fledged stage play was established not only as a regular activity but also as one that was endowed with prestige.

For children who become isolated because of their residence in an institution, it is also essential that program be found which can give them a feeling of being part of the outside community. This is important if the institution by its very design is not to accentuate the feeling of worthlessness and of being unwanted, so characteristic of this group of children.

Drama can be utilized as such an integrating program. The wide outside audience which was stirred by the performance of "Golden Boy" gave not only the cast but the entire campus as well a feeling of being a part of the larger community.

In institutions where large boards and committees and volunteer groups are seeking a function which will bring them in direct contact with the children, the play is a sound contact point.

This brings to mind an experience of a children's receiving home which was faced with the problem of holiday philanthropy, of wide enough concern to have caused the organizing of a conference of representatives from various children's institutions, who met for the purpose of drawing up a list of Do's and Don'ts for holiday giving. This particular agency, too, had been receiving many requests from church groups and other organizations wanting to give parties for these homeless children during the holidays.

As administrators of such institutions are well aware, it is no easy task to interpret to such lay groups the danger that this type of well-meant, service-motivated philanthropy can create or accentuate the feeling of second-class citizenship in these children. As a solution it was decided to try to arrange for these parties to be given *with* the children. Co-operation of a few of these groups was secured to allow the children to put on a show for the adults. The adults were to pay ten cents admission as well as furnish the refreshments. Some of the case workers and teachers interested in the children were also invited.

The show which was presented was a dramatized story about Hallowe'en, featured as part of a Hallowe'en party. Techniques used were those of creative dramatics, since these children ranged in age from six to ten years and were not ready for the more arduous task of producing a formal play.[13]

Our focus in this study is limited to the formal play, but in terms of promoting the children's identification with the community, it is interesting to note some of the results obtained from even this effort, requiring five rehearsals.

After the show, the onrush by all the adults to congratulate the children was unmistakably spontaneous and hearty. There could be little doubt that none of this feeling was forced in a mere attempt to be polite. The children's faces became flushed with success, with the feeling they had really accomplished something. The warm feeling thus generated carried through the rest of the party. The children went on a goblin hunt, played games and charades, and enjoyed refreshments. In marked contrast to the beginning of the evening, before the show, when the adults merely sat in their chairs to watch the children dunking apples and biting doughnuts, they now participated too, joining in the children's laughter and fun. The wall between the adults and the children had come down.

It was heartily agreed that the idea of having the children give a show for the adults in the community was much more beneficial than to have all the giving on the other side. It made the children feel a part of the community and at the same time satisfied the community's philanthropic needs.

In group work agencies a dramatic club lends itself well to integrating functions with other groups and other agencies. The mobile group already mentioned, which grew out of the unmet needs of some of the members of the main theatre group, gave performances for other groups in the community center where it met, as well as for groups outside the agency. A skit was performed for the annual meeting of the Board of Directors of the community center; an arrangement was made whereby skits were exchanged with a Negro group from another neighborhood agency at a Brotherhood Week affair; and the group was called upon by various church, synagogue, and young people's clubs to perform throughout the season.

Community theatres, too, try to develop a close community bond. The idea of combining a play with a party, for example, was used by a Little Theatre Group with which the writer was associated. To this affair were invited such people in the community who could not actively participate in but wanted to feel some identification with the group. Every month a general meeting of the organization would be combined into what was called a Studio Nite. Studio Nites would include the performance of a one-act play or an excerpt from a forthcoming major production, a talk or a demonstration of some related art such as modern dance, a violin solo, followed by refreshments afterward. There were at least one hundred people who would attend these affairs and pay dues into the organization. They had come to think of the group as their own, happy with its successes and concerned with its failures. Their only actual contact was through a Studio Nite.

Social Action Stimulated

Wilson-Ryland mention the potentials for social action contained in drama. They warn, rightfully, against trying to present solutions to problems.[14] "The anger and rebellion belong to the spectator," [15] is John Martin's comment. Drama, as an art, should not make political speeches or exhort people to action. Art is man's interpretation of life, expressed in a way that can be universally recognized and understood. The moment that an exhortation takes place, it ceases to be recognized as experience but becomes propaganda. There may be, of course, a character of a politician or a statesman expounding a point of view. But then all the other sides of this point of view would also have to be expounded, and convincingly so, in order to produce the conflict that is the essence of drama.

The medium of drama can be highly valuable, however, in that it may by revealing the conflict in all its aspects stimulate a great deal of thinking about a problem which may eventually lead to social action.

Stereotypes Broken Down

The attempt to present solutions in plays, to impose a point of view upon an audience, can also lead to the danger of stereotyping characters. This brings to mind a long-running controversy between two persons who were co-directing the play, "Awake and Sing." The controversy concerned the character of Uncle Morty, a rich dress manufacturer. One point of view contended that Uncle Morty was a symbol of the greed and selfishness arising from a society that placed money values above all other values and should, therefore, be portrayed as outright vicious, cruel, and insensitive; otherwise the message of the play might fail to come across.

The other point of view held that Uncle Morty was, first and foremost, a human being and must be so presented if the function of drama as an art were not to be violated. Drama as art cannot be a vehicle for imposing messages. The message, or better still, the education which may result, comes about through the various identifications the audience makes with the various characters. To present a character as a stereotype, all vicious, for example, destroys the possibility of such an identification and calls up, in fact, all the defenses of those individuals in the audience who do not agree with the message.

The second point of view prevailed. Uncle Morty was presented as even pious in places and revealed a sense of humor. And when, in an argument with the old philosophical grandfather, Uncle Morty pointed with deep feeling to the fact that he had worked his way "up from an ice wagon for five dollars a week" to the position he occupied at the present time, and when he pounded on the table, "This is America! put that in your pipe and smoke it!" he was sincere and convincing, and the businessmen in the audience were really bound to him in identification. This is as it should be, for only through identification with one of the characters is there the possibility that what the other characters are saying and representing makes sense too. Thus is there a beginning, perhaps, of social consciousness.

One of the great values of using the creative approach in play production is in its potential of breaking down stereotypes and prejudices. The true creative result of any artistic endeavor, according to Hughes Mearns, is something which has "never happened in the world before." [16] Since the actor starts with himself as a human being, and since each individual human being is unique, the net result of his creation must be something which has "never happened in the world before." Such a unique result is the very opposite of stereotyping.

We have seen an illustration of how working for such a result can be accomplished in the case of the character Scrooge in "A Christmas Carol."

The Use of the Spoken Word

One of the unique aspects of play production is its utilization of the spoken word. There may be more effective means of communication but none so prevalent or so complicated as that of language. The whole human race speaks. It is, in fact, largely due to written and spoken language that the human animal has been able to outstrip the lower forms of animal life.

The complication about words is that they are merely symbols of what they supposedly represent. Our semanticists tell us that words do not accurately reflect all the objects, events, or states of mind at the various times they exist. Nor do they describe the object or event in total. It brings to mind the story of the three blind men who came upon an elephant. A quarrel ensued as to what it was they had encountered. One insisted it was a wall, for he had felt the body; another, a pipe, for he had felt the trunk; another, a snake, for he had felt the tail; but no one, the total elephant. And so it is with words: they convey only a small part of the total meaning.

Another complication in the use of words is that they lend themselves so easily to distortion. Speaking requires so little energy that the insecure person grasps at words in erecting his defenses. Bryng Bryngelson, Director of the Speech Clinic at the University of Minnesota, tells us that such defenses and mechanisms as rationalization, overcompensation, and projection consist of words.[17] It is easy to give a reason for our behavior but not so easy to give the real reason.

Rather than corresponding to our real thoughts and feelings, then, words are often used to distort the real meanings, especially when stigma, shame, and fear are attached to our thoughts, and thereby to the words which would reflect them.

But while words are used to disguise feelings, other forms of communication such as the blush and the flashing eye, the grimace, the tremor of the voice or the sigh, give us away. As Freud says, ". . . mortals are not made to keep a secret . . . self-portrayal oozes from all their pores.." [18]

The genius of an author lies in the fashioning out by the sweat of his brow the combinations of words which will come closest to reflecting the real experiences and feelings he is endeavoring to communicate. There is a proof to the pudding here in the way that these feelings are recognized by the audience, in the universality of the experience. There is a profound truth in the arts in the measure of how feelings and experiences "hit home," how the hearer can see himself. Shakespeare's writings have been preserved these past hundreds of years not because of the pleasing sounds of the words alone but because he was able to express profound human truths which are still valid today. Freud himself went to the arts to illustrate his theories on human behavior.

By being in a play creatively directed, the actor does not memorize lines but studies them in such a way as to get the real thoughts and feelings of the character into his expression of the words. But he cannot substitute somebody else's feelings for his own. In order to get sincerity he must, therefore, get his own feelings and thoughts into the meanings. The art of acting is the communication of the actor's inner thoughts and feelings to the inner thoughts and feelings of the audience through the adept use of the outer media of voice and action. Unless these outer media blend in truthfully with thoughts and feelings, this communication will not be achieved. To hear the ring of sincerity is unmistakable.

To the player there is a great value in getting at words through their association with emotions, for speech is not just a tool of communication. It becomes a part of the person himself. Bryng Bryngelson's definition of speech is as follows:

> . . . a symbolic formulation of an inner emotional state or personal evaluation which operates as a process by which the organism adjusts itself to its environment. In time these symbolic formulations come to control the behavior of the individual.[19]

Teachers of dramatics, English, and speech, as well as social group workers, have a good opportunity through play production with adolescents, when defenses are not yet set within the personality, to ward off the dangers of the kind of talking which is cluttered with artificiality and self-deceit, and to promote clear thinking. Theodor Reik emphasizes thus the importance of the spoken word:

. . . what we think is only what we say within ourselves without pronouncing the words. Everybody has observed that many people make mouth movements as if they would speak when they read and even when they write. The spoken words have an emotional quality different from the words that have only been thought. The Catholic church does not recognize a confession which is only thought or written down. The confession must be *vocalis,* spoken; it must be articulated, vocalized. A comparison between written and thought words shows that the effect of articulate speech is different not only upon the hearer but also upon the speaker himself.[20]

The importance of such verbalization is further expressed by Theodor Reik in the following statement:

It is a true statement that thoughts are speeches not made, or condemned to silence. . . . Thanks to the inner connection between our consciousness and language, an idea formulated in words will be better able to resist the suppressing and repressing forces than one not so formulated. It will be more capable of opposing the tendency to withdraw into the region of the unconscious again. . . .[21]

Expressing a problem in words helps gain a new evaluation of it. And when a person can so express himself and receive understanding from a sympathetic listener, he is helped to become more of a human being and he need not cling so arduously to his defenses.

There has been an interesting study made, as a matter of fact, showing a correlation between the meaningfulness of value words and the strength of values.[22]

Again, we are mindful of the fact that the skill in verbalization one learns by acting in a play does not mean that he is verbalizing or has gained insight into his own particular problem. But because of the insight he has gained into the character's conflicts and his new-found awareness of the universality of problems, he might be stimulated to gain some perspective on himself.

Although it is true that the whole human race speaks, there are some people who have never acquired sufficient skill in the use of words to make them comfortable in social situations depending on this form of communication. What sometimes appears to us as resistance or unfriendliness may be nothing more than a person's inability to state in words what he is thinking or feeling. The constant exercising with lines and meanings that an actor experiences in the preparation of a play can help develop, as it were, a social vocabulary, invaluable as a tool of communication. Such training gives the actor a deep appreciation of the unity of intellectual and emotional communication. It gives him a facility in total communication in which the visual, the emotional, the movement and action all are funneled through the spoken word.

The closer the word fits the thought, the more complete is communication, the more free and spontaneous and genuine is the person, the less hampered and inhibited is he in his relations, the less drain is there on his energy. In a world where one must, in a sense, sell himself before he can sell his goods or his services, sincerity and genuineness and flavor of personality can be most significant. In the words of Bryng Bryngelson, "Adequate speaking bears a direct relationship to emotional security." [23]

FOOTNOTES

1. *The Bulletin of the National Association of Secondary School Principals,* "Dramatics in the Secondary School," Vol. 33, December 1949, No. 166, pp. 2-3.

2. Peter Slade, *Child Drama* (London: University of London Press, Ltd. 1954), Foreword, p. 5.

3. Franz Alexander and Thomas M. French, *Psychoanalytic Therapy* (New York: The Ronald Press, 1946), p. 3.

4. S. R. Slavson, *Recreation and the Total Personality* (New York: Association Press, 1948), p. 90.

5. E. O. Harbin, *The Fun Encyclopedia* (New York-Nashville: Abingdon Press, 1940), p. 8. Used by permission of the publisher.

6. Wendell Johnson, *People in Quandaries* (New York: Harper & Brothers, 1946), p. 12.

7. Editorial in the *New York Herald Tribune,* as cited on book flap of *An Actor Prepares,* by Constantin Stanislavski translated by Elizabeth Reynolds Hapgood (New York: Theatre Arts, Inc., 1936, Copyright 1948 by Elizabeth R. Hapgood). See also Allen Crafton and Jessica Royer, *The Complete Acted Play* (New York: Appleton-Century-Crofts, Inc., 1945), p. 151.

8. Harleigh B. Trecker, *Social Group Work Principles and Practices* (New York: Whiteside, Inc., 1948, Copyright 1955 by Harleigh B. Trecker), p. 86, Revised and Enlarged Edition.

9. William Heard Kilpatrick, *The Project Method* (Teachers College Bulletin, Tenth Series, No. 3, published by Teachers College, Columbia University, New York, October 12, 1918; 9th Impression, March 1925, pp. 11-12.

10. *Ibid.,* March 1925, pp. 11-12. Used by permission of Bureau of Publications, Teachers College, Columbia University.

11. *Ibid.,* p. 18. Used by permission.

12. Dorothea Sullivan, Editor, *The Practice of Group Work,* AASGW (New York: Association Press, 1941), pp. 218-219, "Criteria for Group Work," by Saul Bernstein.

13. A great deal has already been written in this area. Some good reference material follows:

Winifred Ward, *Playmaking with Children* (New York: Appleton-Century-Crofts, Inc., 1947). This book not only describes media and methods used but also contains an excellent annotated bibliography of stories and dramatizations, broken down into age groups from five to fourteen.

C. Lowell Lees, *A Primer of Acting* (New York: Prentice-Hall, Inc., 1940). Although this book is written for adults, it contains many good suggestions for pantomimes and acting exercises which could be used with young children. With young children more action and fewer words is the principle.

S. R. Slavson, *Creative Group Education* (New York: Association Press, 1938). This book contains excellent ideas on the use of creative dramatics in his chapter on drama.

Elizabeth E. Keppie, Conrad F. Wedberg, and Miriam Keslar, *Speech Improvement Through Choral Speaking* (Boston: Expression Company, 1942). This book contains hundreds of play games, "say-ways," "play-ways," tongue twisters, and other devices related to various age groups, which can be helpful in creative dramatics.

Peter Slade, *Child Drama* (London: University of London Press, Ltd., Warwick Square, E.C.4, 1954). This is one of the latest books on the use of this medium. It has been mentioned before in Chapter One.

Gertrude Hartman and Ann Shumaker (Editors for The Progressive Education Association), *Creative Expression* (Milwaukee:

E. M. Hale and Company, 1939). This is one of the oldest books emerging from the progressive education movement. It contains an excellent section called "Creative Expression Through Dramatics" with many suggestions of stories, skits, and plays. It also contains a wide bibliography.

14. Gertrude Wilson and Gladys Ryland, *Social Group Work Practice* (Boston: Houghton Mifflin Company, 1949), p. 301.

15. John Martin, "The Dance," *New York Times,* Theatre Section, Sunday, March 12, 1944, cited by Wilson-Ryland, *op. cit.,* p. 259.

16. Hughes Mearns, *Creative Power* (New York: Doubleday, Doran and Company, 1929).

17. Bryng Bryngelson, "Educating the Emotions and Developing Objective Attitudes Toward the Self," *The Bulletin of the National Association of Secondary School Principals,* Nov. 1945, Vol. 29, No. 133, pp. 39-41.

18. Theodor Reik, *Listening with the Third Ear* (New York: Farrar, Straus and Cudahy, Inc., 1948), p. 23.

19. Bryng Bryngelson, *op. cit.*

20. From *Listening with the Third Ear,* copyright 1948 by Theodor Reik. Permission granted by Farrar, Straus and Cudahy, Inc., publisher.

21. *Ibid.,* p. 208. By permission of the publisher.

22. W. A. Bousfield and Gloria Samborski, "The Relationship Between Strength of Values and the Meaningfulness of Value Words," *Journal of Personality,* Vol. 33, No. 4, Duke University Press, June 1955, pp. 325-381.

23. Bryng Bryngelson, "Applying Hygienic Principles to Speech Problems," *The Quarterly Journal of Speech,* Vol. XXIX, No. 3, October 1943.

CHAPTER ELEVEN

Selecting the Play

IT IS EVIDENT that the play a group selects for production has an important bearing on the social growth to be attained from the activity, important enough to warrant a separate examination.

There is an inclination to avoid material which is too realistic, such as violence, death, brutality, destruction. Plays with happy Hollywood endings seem to be the preference. Indeed, despite the fact that they enjoyed the play and greatly admired the children's performances, certain members of the audience raised questions as to whether the selection of the play "Golden Boy" had been well advised. Isn't there the danger of "stirring up a hornet's nest," was their thoughtful query.

Anticipating such misgivings, the director included on the program a note which read as follows:

> This is a play that presents real problems in real life. There are those who will say that the subject matter is too serious, perhaps too morbid, that entertainment and recreation should be gay, should allow us to forget for the moment the cares of everyday life. But the young people who make up the dramatic club have the conviction that recreation in its finest

sense means to re-create life, to express the disorder of living in an orderly artistic form.

It is our feeling that the conflicts between a father's aspirations and hopes for his child and the child's struggle to be free and independent, the conflict between loyalty and desire, the confusion about success and fame, the struggle to be one's self amidst social and economic pressures, are the conflicts, confusions, and problems of all of us. And if we can objectively understand and genuinely portray the untenable position of Lorna Moon, the frustrations of Mr. Bonaparte, the fears of Mr. Moody, the gnawing ache of Joe Bonaparte—we may move an inch closer toward man's constant, inexorable search for his own fulfillment. In this sense we are inviting you not to be entertained, but to share with the young players a rich experience for which they have tirelessly worked the past five weeks.

Just as we firmly believe that treatment is total, so also is it our conviction that causes for emotional disturbance are multiple and manifold. The case records of many of our unhappy children and families include such factors as vagueness about success, confused values, unrealistic aspirations, unachievable goals—a "reaching for the moon."

If an experience is to result in social growth it needs to include a facing up to the realities of life. Only by knowing what life really is, can we be expected to take a hand in shaping our own destiny.

Concerning this point, Mrs. E. M. Langdon, of the Department of Child Development of the Institute of Education, University of London, says with regard to child drama: "The playing out of things which frighten, confuse or puzzle him is in itself both a form of comfort and reassurance, and a way of moving on towards new attitudes about these things." [1] Those working in the area of play therapy with children have long known the value of this kind of experience. One who has faith in the profound truth of art and in the resilience of human nature will not fear the disclosure of life's realities.

It brings to mind an example that occurred during the preparation of the poignant and stirring one-act play, "Jacob Comes Home," by William Kozlenko. The play ends with as frightening a scene as one can imagine—the delivery of the ashes of Jacob from the Nazis. In the group which was to produce the play was a young, emaciated refugee girl, who had recently lost her entire family to the rapaciousness of these same Nazis. "Jacob Comes Home" almost literally reproduced this experience. The girl overheard her social worker and the director discussing the advisability of her taking part in such a play. The social worker feared that this would reawaken her trauma and her agony, but the director leaned toward the view that reliving her experience in a safe, secure setting might be reassuring to her. The girl settled the controversy by insisting, surprisingly, that she be allowed to read the play, following which she begged to be given a part. There was no evidence that her experience in acting this part had any adverse effect upon her. On the contrary, she seemed to feel a mellowness and relief from this participation.

This example should in no way be understood as a recommended criterion for play selection; that is, the reproduction of the actor's own life experiences. On the contrary, it is best to put some distance between the problem in the play itself and the actor's own situation. In "Golden Boy" the situation of the characters Lorna and Moody was distressingly too close to the actual life involvement of the actors in the first presentation. This would have been avoided if a better casting could have been arranged.

The values and ethics brought out by a play need to be considered, too, in play selection. Such an intensely moving and popular play as "The Valiant" by Holworthy Hall and Robert Middlemass was turned down for production just recently at the treatment center where "Golden Boy" was produced. In another setting the play might have been worth while, but the values and ethics comprising the main theme in the play would have worked against our treatment objectives here. The play glorified the ethic of martyrdom, keeping close-lipped, not betraying a friend, going to one's death with a secret on his lips. Though such courage is admirable under certain circumstances, a treatment center is working, in a way, for opposite goals. It gears its whole program in such a way as to encourage the child's opening up, expressing his secrets, giving up his unrealistic fantasies about life, convincing him he need not feel guilty for recognizing the weaknesses and inadequacies in his own people. In a sense, the play gave sanction to the resistance of the child to treatment. The greatest obstacle to be overcome in order to help unhappy and bewildered children is precisely this resistance to help.

Criteria for play selection should include conflicts that have meaning to the actor, situations which he can associate with his own life experiences and through which he can gain a clearer perspective on the life that surrounds him.

Perhaps a listing of the reasons for the selection of the play "Golden Boy" can help to arrive at more general criteria for play selection.

1. The values stressed were those of being one's self, accepting one's self. It shows the tragedy which can result from unrealistic goals. Such values fall right in line with treatment goals.

2. It offered the opportunity, rather than the danger, of "stirring up a hornet's nest," to "hit home," as it were. It dealt with problems and conflicts of a social nature, with which each member of the cast could feel some identification. The very criteria for a good play or any good piece of art are, in fact, the universality of the problem expressed and the way the members in the audience can identify their feelings with those expressed in the art form.

3. Though such a project as drama has within it always some element of calculated risk as to the possibility of success, the play "Golden Boy" had a certain foolproof quality to it.

Any play as well written as this could have a degree of success if nothing more were accomplished than an intelligent conveyance of the meanings of the lines. Therefore, it offered reasonable certainty of success to the actors.

4. All program activities should take into account what the members want as well as what we think is good for them. Program needs to start where people are, build on what they have, lead from the familiar to the strange. "Golden Boy" dealt with a subject having wide appeal to adolescents, the conflict between boxing and violin playing. The love scenes, too, contained a certain teasing and challenge, emotions which adolescents can handle and portray far more comfortably than they can, for example, tenderness. As was pointed out, the play was an instantaneous, unanimous choice of the youngsters, for it seemed to speak the language of these frustrated youngsters.

5. The language of the streets, made poetic by the author, offered another good starting point for the use of more "literary" drama in the future. It also provided some assurance that lines would be more easily learned and assimilated than language more removed from the adolescent's cultural framework.

6. Basically a melodrama, the play provided many climaxes which gave a number of opportunities for open expression of feeling that was readily understandable and not complicated by too much subtlety.

Each group must, of course, select its play from its own frame of reference and from its own cultural milieu, but it is our experience and our firm belief that plays of the type of "Golden Boy," containing straight, tense drama with emotional appeal, giving opportunities for direct emotional experience with much "telling off," have the best chances for success. If one is not frightened by the subject matter and if one does not underestimate young people's capacity and desire to understand big ideas and complicated characters, the following plays would be suitable for starters:

"Of Mice and Men" by John Steinbeck
"Detective Story" by Sidney Kingsley
"The Crucible" by Arthur Miller
"Beyond the Horizon" by Eugene O'Neill
"Death of a Salesman" by Arthur Miller
"Caine Mutiny Court-Martial" by Herman Wouk
"The Hasty Heart" by John Patrick
"The Rainmaker" by Richard Nash

For adolescents the one-act play is a good introduction to the stimulation of interest in drama. It is short enough so that the sustaining power and frustration tolerance of the participants will not be overtaxed. If one is not afraid to deal with controversial material, "Waiting for Lefty" by Clifford Odets contains stirring material through which adolescents can give vent to their emotions. Eugene O'Neill's sea plays have wide appeal to young people. "The Moon of the Caribbees" and "In the Zone" are tense dramas, as is "The Rope." Other excellent dramas requiring a great deal more sensitivity and understanding, however, are the aforementioned "Jacob Comes Home" by William Kozlenko, "The Rising of the Moon" by Lady Gregory, "The Bishop's Candlesticks" by Norman McKinnel, "Hello Out There" by William Saroyan. "Winterset" by Maxwell Anderson and "Watch on the Rhine" by Lillian Hellman are examples of full-length plays with this quality. The Shakespearean tragedies are possibilities too in groups with drama experience under their belts.

There is an excellent treatment of the subject of one-act plays in Zachar and Kimball's *Plays As Experience*. It contains six one-act plays representing each of the various types of drama, as well as eight other which are labeled "Meeting Personal Problems" and "Understanding Our Democracy." Criteria for play selection in a dramatics program should take into account a balance between the serious and the light. Otherwise a drama group might be typed as one always preoccupied with the grim and bitter—which is, of course, just as undesirable as to be associated only with the frivolous.

However, the most difficult type of play for amateurs to produce is the comedy, especially the sophisticated type such as those written by S. N. Behrman and Philip M. Barrie. A play like "The Male Animal" by James Thurber and Elliot Nugent or "Ah, Wilderness" by Eugene O'Neill are thoughtful and human and offer a good chance for success. As a general rule, however, comedies require a deftness and a preciseness, a certain facility for timing acquired only through a great deal of experience and a great deal of skill in stage techniques. Amateurs should not be overly tempted by what may appear on the surface to be good fun. The farce comedy or the rollicking fantasy such as "The Man Who Married a Dumb Wife" by Anatole France or the classic "A Night at an Inn" by Lord Dunsany can be more profitably undertaken by amateurs. A fantasy such as "The Glittering Gate" by Lord Dunsany, a story of two safecrackers who are attempting to pick the lock of the Gates of Heaven, can introduce a pleasing balance to a dramatics program. "On Borrowed Time" by Paul Osborne or "The Beautiful People" by William Saroyan are excellent full-length fantasies.

A definite experience in human relations can be provided by the folk plays. Lady Gregory's "Spreading the News" is a good example of a hilarious farce of Irish life. "Sunday Costs Five Pesos" by Josephina Niggli is an amusing, well-written Mexican one-act. Her "Tooth or Shave" is a good full-length folk play. "A Marriage Proposal" by Anton Chekhov is an authentic short play of old Russia, as is his full length "The Cherry Orchard."

These, then, are a few of our scattered recommendations of various plays of various types. One final word of caution would be to choose plays that require a royalty payment. The fact that an author has sweated "blood and tears" to wring out the exact phrase that will best portray a thought is some insurance of quality. To be tempted to select a nonroyalty play with the risk of inferior quality is false economy. We shall include in the Bibliography a few carefully edited books of royalty plays.

If one wishes to risk production of a nonroyalty play, William Kozlenko, a master craftsman of the one-act play, has edited a book called *One-Hundred Non-Royalty One-Act Plays*, which might be worth considering.

FOOTNOTE

1. Peter Slade, *Child Drama* (London: University of London Press, Ltd., Warwick Square, E.C.4, 1954), p. 119.

CHAPTER TWELVE

Who Should Do It

NOW THAT WE HAVE ATTEMPTED to show how to direct a play creatively and identified some of the deep and lasting values to be gained therefrom, we come to the crucial question: who should do it? The creative processes described and the objectives to be attained are a merging of art and social service. Much of the skill in the one is the skill of the other. Indeed, there is art in social service and certainly there is social growth in art. Sybil Thorndike describes acting in this way: "Acting . . . is . . . an art which can help to build human beings into something better and more understanding than they are by nature—to build them into sensitive creatures able to feel the sorrows and joys of others as their own." [1]

Never do we have enough knowledge about anything, let alone enough about art and human behavior. Up until the day they died Stanislavski, the artist, and Freud, the analyst, were not satisfied that they knew enough. And only death halted their continued efforts to know more.

Nevertheless, were we to wait for all the data to come in, nothing would be attempted. But perhaps there is some point in trying to arrive at a distinction between what one needs to know in order to get started and what one can continue to learn as he experiments. For that reason it may be helpful to pull together here some of the various skills and knowledge one needs to have in order to undertake the creative direction of a play.

Technical Drama Skills

1. Acting

In directing amateur plays with inexperienced casts, the director is much more of a teacher than is the professional director. He need not necessarily be superior in the art of acting than some of his cast members, but he must be prepared to make concrete suggestions, to demonstrate actions and movement.

2. Internal Techniques of Acting

Not only must the director know what the internal techniques of acting are, but he also should himself have a good retentive memory which can serve as a storehouse of experiences upon which he can draw for his creativity. He needs the kind of recall memory in which impressions are vivid.

3. Sense of Focus

Knowing how to "point up" action and being aware of what attracts and what distracts in terms of stage positions, movement, voice, and so on, are essential in the director's body of knowledge. A sense of timing would also be included here. Knowledge of stage composition, too, is necessary—how to place people on stage so that everything can be seen readily and with the proper focus.

4. Reading

He must know how to phrase, how to ferret out varying thoughts, how to extract the maximum meanings from lines.

5. *Voice*

A minimum knowledge of voice anatomy—stomach muscles, diaphragmatic breathing, resonators—is necessary in order to help actors be heard (project their lines out into the audience) without ruining their voices. The director should know a few good voice exercises.

6. *Imagery*

The skill in the sounding of words according to the way they look is also valuable.

7. *Blocking*

The art of picturing movements to fit lines is basic. The director needs to go through a play many times in advance in order to place the sequence of his stage pictures, that is, the way in which the characters will group themselves on the stage, on what line they will turn, stand, and move. The beginning director should actually chart all this out in a prompt book before he gets started. Though he may make many changes as he goes along, this will give him something with which to start.

The writer in directing the two illustrations presented here indulged in spot blocking; in other words, he was prepared with only a few basic positions and relied on the action of the moment to guide him in his blocking. For the beginning director this would be risky, for if he groped and floundered too much for the proper movements and action on the spot, rehearsals might become laborious.

8. *Paraphrasing*

A good imagination is needed in order to be adept at paraphrasing lines and thoughts as needed.

9. *Emotional Build-Up*

The director must have a sense of climax, a knowledge of how to build up to the climaxes with volume, pace, variety.

He must, therefore, know the structure of a play, the exposition, rising action, climax, falling action, and the like.

10. Keen Observation

He must be able to pick out "bits" of action, mannerisms, gestures, and must have good judgment as to whether these help or hinder.

11. Stage "Business"

The director needs to help actors dissipate nervous energy, give them things to do with their hands. He must also have a sense of economy of action and movement, an element of all art. There should be no waste motion. Nothing should happen which does not fulfill a purposeful function.

12. A Sense of Aesthetic Distance

Having a sense of empathy, knowing when emotions or actions have gone overboard, is essential. The illustration in Chapter Eight of Roxy sneering "So what!" at Mr. Bonaparte is an example in which the director felt a distressing empathy.

13. A Sense of Symbol

The director must sense dramatic possibilities in symbols —a door, a chair, a report card, a train arriving on time. In "Golden Boy" it was a car that led Joe on to glittering heights and it was the car that destroyed him.

14. Pacing and Tone

A play may require a peppy pace with a rather boisterous tone, as in "The Man Who Came to Dinner," while another may need to be played more leisurely, with whimsy, like the fantasy "On Borrowed Time."

15. Motivation

This skill mainly involves knowledge of human behavior, but there is also a technical aspect to it requiring a facility in sensing possibilities in movement and stage position to help portray a motive. Motivation here is used as a verb. Directors and actors develop a certain inventiveness and ingenuity for motivating an action. They may heave a sigh of disgust in order to sit down. We like to relate the incident where an actor fell asleep on the stage between acts. Unnoticed as the curtains were opened, the actor found himself under the bright lights facing the audience, with no purpose on the stage. Assuming his stage character of an argumentative racketeer, he grunted to the left wing and stalked out the right, giving the impression he had just made his final point to an imaginary opponent off stage.

16. Discussion Leading

We point to this as a technical skill, since so much of the creative process includes discussion with the cast, helping the members to bring out their ideas. Social group workers all have this skill in common.

17. Use of Peripheral Skills

There are peripheral skills such as *make-up, construction, scene design, costuming, lighting.* Although these can be delegated to experts, the director needs to know enough about them to recognize if their functions are being fulfilled adequately. Securing *advertisements* for programs might be added to this list.

18. Group Processes

More than anyone else on the production staff, the director must know the acting that goes on between the lines. He must sense and observe critically how one character *listens* to what another character says, reacts to him, is moved by him; and he must know whether these reactions are psychologically sound and dramatically effective. He needs to be able to note and analyze the group ensemble work. (See the section on Stage Interinfluence, in Chapter Two.)

Literary and Critical Ability

Though we have attempted to spell out some of the technical skills in drama needed to direct plays, others are too intangible to lend themselves to classification. We can only say that if one is to direct a play, he needs to be able to analyze it, formulate the theme, grasp its ideas, recognize its wisdom. In order to do this successfully, he needs a broad foundation in the liberal arts. He must know literature, acquire a distinct taste of his own, possess good critical faculties.

Leadership Quality

We feel about leadership like Pontius Pilate, who asked what is truth and did not stay for the answer. Books have been written which have attempted to define this quality. It is evident that a director needs this ability in leadership. He needs to be able to speak freely with people and to move easily among them. He must inspire confidence and enable his actors to be free to express themselves. Because he deals with a production staff with a wide variety of assignments, he must be a good organizer and a wise administrator, allowing his staff to achieve their own creative satisfactions out of their jobs and to carry out their assignments with trust and confidence and a minimum of encumbrances. While he needs a good eye for detail, he should not become like the centipede, who functioned well until he began analyzing how each leg moved separately. The director should not get personally immersed in all the minutiae of production. The writer remembers vividly an incident where a director who had particular skill and interest in the art of make-up spent days getting a specially made eyelid to look exactly right when he could have spent the time more profitably elsewhere. If anyone, it is the director who needs to keep the focus on the totality of the undertaking and to keep a sense of balance and of relative values in all the efforts expended.

Knowledge of Human Behavior, Human Nature, and Life

When the writer asked a prominent director what he thought
was his greatest area of knowledge and skill in play direction, he promptly replied, "Human behavior." Surely it is
clear that if one is to portray human behavior lifelike on a
stage, he must first understand this behavior. Here indeed is
where the skills of the art of drama and the behavioral sciences merge. Here is where these fields can share and learn
from each other. While the area of knowledge is the same, the
purposes and motivations for acquiring this skill may differ.
The social worker, the psychologist, or the psychiatrist seeks
such knowledge in order to help his client with personal
problems. The teacher seeks to know her pupils in order best
to help them grow socially, emotionally, and intellectually.
The social researcher seeks such knowledge in order to clas-
sify it.

The drama director is interested in human behavior almost
for its own sake. He is attuned to the sights, sounds, smells,
and movements of human behavior. He may have taken a
course in psychology, here or there, but his primary method
of learning behavior is through observation and through the
recording of these observations as indelible impressions on
his mind and in his storehouse of memories, for he is a person who never ceases to marvel at life's wonders. He can
be as fascinated by an unusual display on the grocery shelves
as he is by a violent accident. He can be equally drawn to
brawny, unshaven truck drivers as he can to slick, sophisticated executives. It is this capacity to be interested in the
world around him and to enjoy life's simplest adornments
that a would-be director must possess to bring imagination
and lifelike qualities to the direction of his plays. The intellectual who becomes readily bored is not a good candidate
for play direction.

To the Would-Be Director

If one has the will to try directing, let not the list of needed skills look so overwhelming that one would be deterred from play production. Much of the knowledge listed comes from the play itself. The lines give clues to understanding character and action and reaction. The way to go about learning how to direct a play is first to find out all one can about directing and plays. One should become a theatre goer and practice writing critiques. One should observe someone else direct a play, perhaps by approaching the community theatre director and volunteering to be his assistant. When one feels comfortable enough, then he may try it himself under competent supervision. After some such experience, and if one gains confidence, he might try going it alone. And if he makes mistakes the first time, he will learn from them for the next attempt. Perfection in art is never attained.

From Where Will the Social Dramatists Come?

Who the social dramatists of the future will be and from what fields of study they will come is not for us to prophesy. Perhaps they will come from the drama schools, those drama majors who are interested in human welfare and will find in the schools or in the various social service fields opportunities to use their dramatic talents and skills to help people grow. Or perhaps there may be some psychologists or social workers who have a flair for drama and an interest in it who may see this as a good program tool with which to practice their professions.

We believe, however, that when there is ample recognition of a job to be done that is important and worth while, the people to do it will come forth. Agnes Meyer proclaims that the vital task of responsible social leadership today is one "that will help people achieve their own unique personalities through relationship to a meaningful world . . ." [2]

It is our hope that this book has shown how participation in play production can help in achieving this aim. No one can learn play direction by reading a book. But if we have succeeded in stimulating interest in play production and if we have promoted some recognition of the potency of this program tool in giving people a new-found awareness of their own dignity with their own "unique personalities through relationship to a meaningful world," the aim of the book will have been accomplished.

For Future Study and Experimentation

We suggest the following two areas for future study and experiment with the tool of play production:

1. *The Use of Play Production for Therapy*

The result of the experiment with the project of "Golden Boy" showed that as a group activity, play production could be successfully achieved in a resident treatment center with adolescents. This is a necessary first step in any more intensive work with this medium. The experiment also produced some indications that projects of this type could offer, perhaps, an avenue to therapy for selected individuals. What remains to be explored further is this latter aspect of the use of play production as a stimulant to therapy, the ultimate goal of resident treatment. In doing so, a great deal of time would need to be allotted to solving not only the design of such a research but also the very mechanics of communication between the members of the therapeutic team. It would be necessary for all members of the staff so concerned to have a voice in the selection of the play, to study the play thoroughly so as to be familiar with the conflicts, themes, and the characters, to help match the players and the parts in terms of the therapeutic indications, and to meet regularly with the director to exchange significant information and to study together the therapeutic impact emanating from the play.

Perhaps such study and experimentation can exploit more systematically and scientifically the use of play production in opening new pathways toward greater self-awareness and insight. In treatment centers for disturbed children as well as in mental hospitals, such activity might become a means whereby patients could be helped to get a better hold of reality and to regain their self-respect and courage. There are hospitals already experimenting with this medium, as has been noted in the Preface.

2. *The Use of Play Production for the Teaching of Human Behavior*

It is evident by this time that a vast amount of human behavior is learned attendant upon the preparation for the portrayal of a character upon the stage. We submit that such activity would be of great value to students in such human behavior classes as social work, clinical and social psychology, educational guidance, vocational counseling, for this activity adds a new dimension to the understanding of people. It goes beyond the learning of the nomenclature, the classifications, the given terms of human behavior. It teaches the behavior itself. It gives one an experience in attuning himself to the sights, sounds, smells, and movements of behavior. It teaches one not only to understand behavior but also to "feel the joys and sorrows of others as their own." [3] Surely those working in the helping professions agree to the need of empathizing with a client.

It is not the mere reading of a play followed by discussion that is being advocated for experiment here. It is the full process—the casting, acting, and carrying out of a production that should be tried in order to extract the maximum learning from such an experience. It need not be an elaborate affair, to be sure. Its presentation for a school social get-together would suffice. But the acting of a character added to discussion, analysis, and perhaps relating it to the terms of behavior would in the words of Mary Parker Follett "keep the man whole," "find out what he is really doing," and teach us that

> . . . the ideas of people are not formed in their "minds" as conceptual pictures, but depend on their activities. . . . Concepts can never be presented to me merely, they must be knitted into the structure of my being, and this can be done only through my own activity.[4]

FOOTNOTES

1. Peter Slade, *Child Drama* (London: University of London Press, Ltd., Warwick Square, E.C.4, 1954), p. 5.

2. Agnes E. Meyer, "No Man Is an Island," *Social Work*, Vol. I, No. 3, July 1956, p. 5.

3. Peter Slade, *op. cit.*, p. 5.

4. M. P. Follett, *Creative Experience* (New York: Longmans, Green & Company, 1930), p. 151.

Bibliography

Books of Plays

Cerf, Bennett and Cartmell, Van H. (editors), *Sixteen Famous American Plays* (New York: Random House, Inc., 1941).

Cerf, Bennett and Cartmell, Van H. (editors), *Sixteen Famous British Plays* (New York: Random House, Inc., 1942).

Cerf, Bennett and Cartmell, Van H. (editors), *Sixteen Famous European Plays* (New York: Random House, Inc., 1943).

Cerf, Bennett and Cartmell, Van H. (editors), *Thirty Famous One-Act Plays,* The Modern Library (New York: Random House, Inc., 1949), 617 pp.

Gassner, John (editor), *Best American Plays, Third Series (1945–51)* (New York: Crown Publishers, 1952).

Gassner, John (editor), *Best Plays of the Modern American Theatre, Second Series* (New York: Crown Publishers, 1947), 774 pp.

Gassner, John (editor), *Twenty Best Plays of the Modern American Theatre* (New York: Crown Publishers, 1939), 874 pp.

Kozlenko, William (editor), *One-Hundred Non-Royalty One-Act Plays* (New York: Grosset & Dunlap, 1940).

Zachar, Irwin J. and Kimball, Rodney A. (editors), *Plays As Experience* (New York: The Odyssey Press, 1944), 369 pp.

Drama and Speech

Albright, H. D., et al., *Principles of Theatre Art* (Cambridge, Mass.: Riverside Press, 1955), 546 pp.

Bryngelson, Bryng, "Applying Hygienic Principles to Speech Problems," *The Quarterly Journal of Speech,* Vol. XXIX, No. 3, October 1943.

Bryngelson, Bryng, "Educating the Emotions and Developing Objective Attitudes Toward the Self," *The Bulletin of the National Association of Secondary School Principals,* Nov. 1945, Vol. 29, No. 133.

Cole, Toby (compiler), *Acting: A Handbook of the Stanislavski Method* (New York: Crown Publishers, 1947, 1955), 223 pp.

Crafton, Allen and Royer, Jessica, *The Complete Acted Play* (New York: Appleton-Century-Crofts, Inc., 1945), 385 pp.

Dean, Alexander, *Fundamentals of Play Directing* (New York: Farrar and Rinehart, Inc., 1941).

Dolman, John, Jr., *The Art of Play Production* (New York: Harper & Brothers, 1940), 421 pp.

"Dramatics in the Secondary School," *The Bulletin of the National Association of Secondary School Principals,* Vol. 33, No. 166, December 1949.

Evans, Dina Reese, *Changes in Social Behavior and Emotional Attitudes of High School Students Participating in Dramatic Art in the High Schools of Cleveland Heights, Ohio.* A thesis submitted in partial fulfillment of the requirements for the Degree of Doctor of Philosophy, in the Department of Speech, in the Graduate College of the State University of Iowa, August 1932.

Gassner, John, *Producing the Play* (New York: The Dryden Press, 1941 and 1953), 744 pp.

Harbin, E. O., *The Fun Encyclopedia* (New York: Abingdon Press, 1940), "Fun with Dramatics," pp. 517-547.

Hartman, Gertrude and Shumaker, Ann (editors for The Progressive Education Association), *Creative Expression* (Milwaukee: E. M. Hale and Company, 1939), 350 pp.

Johnson, Wendell, *People in Quandaries* (New York: Harper & Brothers, 1946), 532 pp.

Keppie, Elizabeth E., Wedberg, Conrad F., and Keslar, Miriam, *Speech Improvement Through Choral Speaking* (Boston: Expression Company, 1942), 277 pp.

Lees, C. Lowell, *A Primer of Acting* (New York: Prentice-Hall, Inc., 1940), 180 pp.

Martin, John, "The Dance" (a column), *New York Times Theatre Section*, Sunday, March 12, 1944.

Peck, Seymour, "The Temple of 'The Method,' " *The New York Times Magazine*, Section 6, Part 1, May 6, 1956, p. 26.

Selden, Samuel, *The Stage in Action* (New York: F. S. Crofts & Co., 1946), 324 pp.

Sievers, W. David, "Autopsy on 'The Group,' " *The Quarterly Journal of Speech*, December 1949.

Slade, Peter, *Child Drama* (London: University of London Press, Ltd., Warwick Square, E.C.4, 1954), 379 pp.

Stanislavski, Constantin, *An Actor Prepares*, translated by Elizabeth Reynolds Hapgood (New York: Theatre Arts, Inc., 1945), 295 pp.

Stanislavski, Constantin, *Building a Character*, translated by Elizabeth Reynolds Hapgood (New York: Theatre Arts Books: Robert M. MacGregor, 1949), 292 pp.

"Theatrical Therapy," from section under "Medicine" in *Time* Magazine, March 28, 1955, pp. 94-95.

Ward, Winifred, *Playmaking with Children* (New York: Appleton-Century-Crofts, Inc., 1947), 312 pp.

General Human Relations

Alexander, Franz and French, Thomas Morton, *Psychoanalytic Therapy* (New York: The Ronald Press Company, 1946), 353 pp.

Bousfield, W. A. and Samborski, Gloria, "The Relationship Between Strength of Values and the Meaningfulness of Value Words," *Journal of Personality*, Vol. 33, No. 4, Duke University Press, June 1955, pp. 325-381.

Coyle, Grace L., *Group Work with American Youth* (New York: Harper & Brothers, 1948), 270 pp.

Follett, M. P., *Creative Experience* (New York: Longmans, Green & Company, 1930), 303 pp.

Hailman, David B., "A Code of Ethics for the Social Worker," *Social Work Journal*, Vol. 30, No. 2, April 1949.

Hamilton, Gordon, *Theory and Practice of Social Case Work* (New York: Columbia University Press, 1940), 388 pp.

Kilpatrick, William Heard, *The Project Method*, Teachers College Bulletin, Tenth Series, No. 3, published by Teachers College, Columbia University, New York, October 12, 1918; 9th Impression, March 1925.

Mearns, Hughes, *Creative Power* (New York: Doubleday & Company, 1929).

Meyer, Agnes E., "No Man Is an Island," *Social Work,* Vol. 1, No. 3, July 1956, pp. 3-10.

Redl, Fritz and Wineman, David, *Children Who Hate* (Glencoe, Ill.: Free Press, 1951).

Redl, Fritz and Wineman, David, *Controls from Within* (Glencoe, Ill.: Free Press, 1952), 332 pp.

Reik, Theodor, *Listening with the Third Ear* (New York: Farrar, Straus and Cudahy, Inc., 1948), 514 pp.

Slavson, S. R., *Creative Group Education* (New York: Association Press, 1938).

Slavson, S. R., *Recreation and the Total Personality* (New York: Association Press, 1948), 205 pp.

Slavson, S. R., *Re-educating the Delinquent* (New York: Harper & Brothers, 1954), 251 pp.

Sullivan, Dorothea (editor), *The Practice of Group Work* (New York: Association Press, 1941).

Trecker, Harleigh B., *Social Group Work Principles and Practices* (New York: Whiteside Press, 1948; Revised and Enlarged Edition, copyright 1955 by Harleigh B. Trecker), 442 pp.

Wilson, Gertrude and Ryland, Gladys, *Social Group Work Practice* (Boston: Houghton Mifflin Company, 1949), 687 pp.

Wittenberg, Rudolph M., *So You Want to Help People* (New York: Association Press, 1947), 174 pp.